THE GREAT
SCHOOL RETHINK

THE GREAT
SCHOOL RETHINK

FREDERICK M. HESS

Harvard Education Press
Cambridge, Massachusetts

Paperback ISBN 978-1-68253-810-4.

Library of Congress Cataloging-in-Publication Data is on file.

Published by Harvard Education Press,
an imprint of the Harvard Education Publishing Group
Harvard Education Press
8 Story Street
Cambridge, MA 02138

Cover Design: Wilcox Design
Cover Image: dylan_burrill/iStock.com

The typefaces in this book are Minion Pro and Myriad Pro

For Gray and Blake: May your schools be places of imagination, excellence, love, and wonder.

Contents

Preface

I didn't want to write this book.

Yeah, I know, I know. But lots of experts have penned lots of books offering lots of recipes for reforming schools. I wasn't eager to add to that pile, even after the dislocations of COVID-19. Worse, when funders, advocates, and the US Secretary of Education started burbling about the need for a post-pandemic "Great Reset," the grandiose rhetoric (and cavalier confidence that they knew just *how* things should be "reset") left me cold.

If you're not familiar with my thinking, I've always been skeptical of ambitious, sweeping reform projects. I was never a big fan of No Child Left Behind, Race to the Top, or the Common Core. As I wrote several years ago, in *Letters to a Young Education Reformer*:

> I'm more interested in stripping away anachronistic policies and empowering educators than in imposing my preferred practices and programs. That's because I think the best-designed and most promising solutions will come from educators and entrepreneurs on the ground, and not from reformers ensconced in office buildings in state capitals or Washington, D.C. I see reform less as a roster of fixes to be imposed and more as a dynamic process of reinvention, evolution, and support for those doing the work.[1]

I didn't want to write a book promising the kind of pat recipes I usually lampoon. After all, I've never been a school or system leader. There are others who know far more about technology than I do. I don't evaluate programs, and I'm always hesitant to insist that *this* tutoring program or *that* new curriculum will do wonders.

Given all that, why the heck *did* I wind up writing this book? Well, I thought a bit more.

When schools across the land closed their doors in March 2020, it was the greatest shock that American education had ever experienced. As families, communities, and neighborhoods dealt with the fallout, many things became newly clear. Too much school time gets wasted. The parent-school relationship has grown distant. Families need more and better school options. Schools are too inflexible and don't make good use of new technologies.

None of this means that school leaders or public officials need another eleven-point plan (with colorful PowerPoint slides) from on high. And it sure doesn't mean they need some Great Reset. But it does make it a good time to ask hard questions about how schools use time and talent, what they do with digital tools, and how they work with parents.

After some reflection, I concluded that I might have something to offer after all. I've spent a couple of decades engaging on just these questions with teachers, school and system leaders, policy makers, union chiefs, tech entrepreneurs, influential researchers, and deep-pocketed funders. During the decade-plus I've penned *Education Week*'s "Rick Hess Straight Up" column, I've interviewed and learned from hundreds of educators, entrepreneurs, and scholars about the kinds of staffing and technological challenges that schools are wrestling with today.

I've taken hard looks at a slew of reforms, new programs, and models, and talked to the individuals who've developed them. Heck, a few years back, I got tagged as the "grumpy uncle of school reform." I've always tried to speak bluntly about both the possibilities and shortcomings of school improvement strategies, as well as what it takes for them to deliver.

I've spent a lot of years teaching, speaking to, and working with school and system leaders, teachers, and policy makers, helping them sort through problems and points of confusion. I've developed lessons to help them wrestle with the kinds of challenges that the pandemic brought to the fore. The more I thought about it, the more writing this book felt like an opportunity to distill much of what I've shared in so many other forums.

I may not have a prescription for a Great Reset, but I don't think we need one. Indeed, I fear the search for the grand solution has helped fuel the spinning of wheels that has yielded—to quote the great education scholar Charles Payne—"so much reform, so little change."[2]

And, having experienced the pandemic as a dad with two young, school-age kids, my professional cool was tempered by parental frustration. Watching schools struggle to answer the challenges of a once-in-a-century cataclysm highlighted and exacerbated longtime frailties. Overburdened teachers. Disengaged students. Impersonal education technology. A lack of transparency. A chasm between time spent in school and time spent learning. A need for more family-friendly options. Strained parent-school relationships.

As I pondered the opportunities to do better, it struck me that there's less need for a Great Reset than a great *rethink*. Instead of more self-assured answers, there might be more value in helping to ensure that we're asking the right questions. If that impulse doesn't come naturally to many of those passionately seeking to improve schools, that just may make it all the more necessary.

WHY RETHINK?

The moment I start talking about the need for a "rethink," many in the audience quite reasonably ask, "What exactly do you mean by 'rethinking'?" Or, "So, how do you want schools to change?" Or, "Is there a hidden agenda here?"

These are the fairest of questions. I'll answer as best I can.

For starters, lots of sensible education leaders, parents, and teachers are leery of talk about rethinking. I get it. I do. I mean, my inbox is filled most days with press releases from corporate flacks who say things like, "We live in a digitized 2.0 Bitcoin-Netflix-Uber-DoorDash world and schools need to compete by RETHINKING to leverage cognitive connectivity and hyper-personalized nanotechnology." This stuff is both icky and banal. But it's a mistake to be unduly distracted by the quacks and the charlatans. They can borrow some of these words, but that doesn't give them custody of the ideas.

So, what do *I* mean when I talk about rethinking? Well, schools are organized today in ways that waste time, overburden educators, misuse technology, and alienate parents. Worse, schools too often take the most human and heartfelt of acts—the mentoring of kids and sharing of knowledge—and turn them into drudgery. Rethinking isn't merely about asking how to do the same things better, but how to liberate kids from tedium and educators from pointless tasks and paperwork. It entails asking how new tools can offer students richer experiences, how schools can more fully partner with parents, and how students can spend more time engaging with skilled teachers and stimulating mentors.

How do I want schools to change? I want kids to play more games, master more rigorous math, read more fiction, engage in more debates, play more music, and learn more history. I want schools to be both more rigorous and more joyous. I want more assurance that seven-year-olds are mastering the building blocks of literacy and more freedom for seventeen-year-olds to be out in the world learning a trade. I want schools to find ways to do vastly better with struggling students *and* with high achievers. I want teachers to have more control over their profession and more freedom to focus on the things that matter for kids.

As I said, I don't claim to have any pat recipes for making this happen. That's why I offer a rethink rather than a reset. Resets start with recipes; rethinking with the right questions about what comes next.

Authors who write books like this are usually making the case for specific programs, policies, or projects. Here, while I'll discuss particular endeavors at various points, my intent is *not* to suggest "you've got to do *this*," but to ask what we can learn from these models.

Do I have a hidden agenda in all of this? Well, for starters, I'm not at all concerned with whether rethinking unfolds in traditional district schools, charter schools, private schools, or homeschools. I'm also not concerned with whether it's remote or in-person or whether it gets labeled "cutting-edge" or "old-fashioned." And I'm certainly not worried about whether it fits existing teacher-of-record requirements or job descriptions.

The aim is not just for schools to do better, but to give those who work in and around them permission to imagine how schooling can be made more human, challenging, and exhilarating.

For better or worse, *that's* my agenda.

A Word About the Exercises

At various points in the pages that follow, readers will encounter exercises in boxes like this one. These are lessons I've developed and used over the years in teaching school and system leaders, teachers, graduate students, advocates, and community leaders. The exercises are intended to provide an opportunity for readers to engage with the ideas we're discussing and put their own thoughts to work.

You'll notice that the exercises are written for groups rather than for the individual reader. I know that's unusual (to say the least). But it reflects my conviction that rethinking is a collaborative endeavor, not an individual one. It requires shared reflection and active problem-solving. Unfortunately, would-be reformers are too often prone to view school improvement as a technical challenge, as if it's a matter of who can dream up the "best" idea.

Here's the problem: pondering an exercise by oneself makes it just too easy to get caught up in cool-sounding ideas and skip past the rules, realities, routines, and competing demands that make schools work the way they do. In short, while *thinking* is a solo activity, *rethinking* requires collaboration.

I've found that the exercises tend to work pretty well regardless of whether participants are novice teachers or seasoned education leaders. They'll play out differently depending on the group, but there's consistent value benefit (regardless of role or experience) in linking unfamiliar ideas to the more familiar realities of schools and classrooms. That's true for both wide-eyed novices and experienced educators.

Readers will find three kinds of exercises in the pages that follow:

Check Your Understanding. These exercises ask participants to answer questions about schooling. The point isn't to guess the right answers but to ponder what we know and what we don't. The trick is ensuring that participants don't pull out their phones and Google the answers, which defeats the purpose by stripping out the reflection and conversation.

Take a Step Back. These exercises invite readers to pause and examine rules or routines by thinking about them in a different context. Some involve comparing how we structure things in schooling to how they're ordered in different fields. Others involve trying to view education challenges through an unaccustomed lens.

Imagine If. In these exercises, participants are asked to wrestle with new possibilities. The goal is to stretch their sense of what might be done, so that school improvement is framed by discussion of what's promising rather than what's permitted.

A general note for those conducting these exercises virtually: most of these translate pretty cleanly to an online format. When exercises call for groups or pairings, you can simply substitute breakout rooms. If an exercise calls for groups to share their responses or ideas with the whole group, replace chart paper and markers with a Google Slides presentation.

ASKING BOTH "WHY?" AND "WHY NOT?"

More than a half-century ago, as he pursued the presidency during a time of frustration, rage, and turmoil, Robert F. Kennedy famously declared, "Some men see things as they are, and say why. I dream of things that never were, and say why not." It's a sentiment that's as timely now as it was then. It's also a mantra for rethinking—well, half a mantra anyway. That's because, at least when it comes to schooling, asking "Why not?" about the things that never were requires *also* asking "Why?" about the things that are.

Look, the easiest thing in the world to do is *talk* about school improvement. It's a whole lot easier to write white papers, deliver keynotes, and churn out colorful PowerPoints than to change things in real schools for real kids.

So, nothing here should be taken to suggest that fresh thinking is a substitute for rolling up our sleeves. The point, rather, is to empower educators to do the hard stuff by better leveraging the tools they possess, more thoughtfully utilizing school staff, and more fully meeting the needs of students and families.

Schools and school systems are such a habitual part of our lives that we can forget to ask basic questions: Why do high schools organize courses like they do? Why do school calendars look like they do? Why does a teacher's job look like it does? Why do new learning technologies keep disappointing us? Why do so many parents feel disconnected from their schools?

Rethinking is about imagining the new while remaining grounded in an understanding of the old. It requires looking both backward and forward, with an appreciation of how things really are and what they could be.

CHAPTER 1

The Great School Disruption

U ntil March 2020, American schooling looked much as it had in 1920. Despite new technologies, ever-increasing outlays, and wave upon wave of reform, the rhythms and routines of America's schools were little changed. Students set out from their homes in the early morning, sat in front of a single teacher or series of teachers, sporadically used the latest technologies, and then headed home. Dress codes, popular pedagogies, the number of adults in the building, and the technology changed, but what students and teachers actually *do* all day had not.

Then came COVID-19. Schools shuttered across the nation, forcing educators and families to scramble. The sudden shift to remote learning spurred new practices and led teachers to explore new skills and attempt new strategies. The pandemic altered household routines and upended how tens of millions of families interacted with schools. And it gave families an unparalleled window into what happens during the school day.

Even as the pandemic receded, disruption lingered. Students had suffered staggering learning loss. Behavioral and disciplinary issues were rampant. Enrollment in the nation's public schools declined by more than one million students, the biggest drop ever recorded. In New York City, the nation's largest school district, enrollment fell by *a quarter*, from more than a million students to 760,000.[1] Schools were plagued by widespread staffing challenges. Interest in homeschooling and other alternatives exploded. All of this loosened the status quo's grip on school norms, parent expectations, and the public imagination.

The upshot: the pandemic aggravated and illuminated frustrations that had long been simmering in American education. At the same time, the disruption born of this once-in-a-century pandemic made for an extraordinary opportunity to rethink K–12 schooling.

Unfortunately, as school systems spent vast sums to address COVID-19 and its aftermath, the responses were all too familiar: add staff, buy tablets, seek "better" curricula, and chase the latest instructional fad. For decades, advocates have tried a host of similar reforms. In recent years, three of the most prominent were pushes to revamp teacher evaluation, promote new academic standards, and pursue ambitious "school-turnaround" strategies. The results were consistently disappointing.

In 2018, a seven-year evaluation of the Bill & Melinda Gates Foundation's $575 million Intensive Partnerships for Effective Teaching initiative, the crown jewel of a sweeping national push to overhaul teacher evaluation, concluded that the effort failed to boost student achievement, attract talented teachers, or even change the results of teacher evaluation.[2] The ambitious, controversial Common Core State Standards ultimately had no impact on student achievement.[3] A massive federal study concluded that the billions spent on the federal School Improvement Grant program hadn't improved student outcomes.[4]

I could go on. But I'll spare you the litany.[5]

Meanwhile, there are pressing challenges that need to be addressed. The performance of American students has long been mediocre, at best, on international assessments. In 2019, even before the devastation of the pandemic, two of three fourth graders were rated below "proficient" in reading on the National Assessment of Educational Progress (NAEP).[6] The NAEP also makes clear that reading and math performance had plateaued for a decade before the pandemic ever hit. Huge numbers of students are disengaged, especially in high school. A troubling number of youth reported feeling lonely and anxious even before COVID-19, and those numbers skyrocketed during the pandemic.[7] Parents report feeling disconnected from schools.[8]

Obviously, there is a raft of problems to solve.

For all that, the pages ahead offer no grand, unified agenda for solving them. I know that's not the way this is usually done. Most books of this ilk set out, understandably, with clear solutions in mind. If they address the use of time, it's because they're calling for an extended school day, a longer school year, or a new model of scheduling. If they address school choice, it's because they're out to make the case for or against it.

Such an approach has value. But it also has limitations. The recommendations only rarely work as advertised. In some schools or communities, they may not even be feasible. The emphasis on prescribed answers can make it harder to ask critical questions. And a prefab agenda can make it tougher for educators, parents, or community leaders to focus on forging solutions that meet their specific circumstances.

I'm more interested in what educators *might* do rather than what they must do, across schools and communities with very different needs. How might they look anew at the use of time, talent, and technology? How might they rethink the role of choice or the relationship between schools and families? In a nutshell, to the extent I have an agenda here, it's to expand the realm of what's possible when it comes to school improvement.[9]

PUNCTUATED EQUILIBRIUM

Despite the dismal track record of so many high-profile reforms, the faith that "more is better" has long been an organizing principle of school improvement. Even though after-inflation, per-pupil spending nearly tripled over the past half-century, there's a widespread conviction that more funding will make all the difference.[10] Even as school employees increased at a rate that far outstripped enrollment, there's an insistence that more staff are needed.[11] Even as one technology after another disappoints, loud voices insist that the next time will be different.

All this activity hasn't yielded much in the way of substantive change. And yet, while inertia may be the rule in schooling (as in so much of life), there are pivotal moments when disruption can spur meaningful change— moments of *punctuated equilibrium.*

Evolutionary biologists Stephen Jay Gould and Niles Eldredge coined the term "punctuated equilibrium" in 1972 to describe those times when massive disruptions trigger a burst of evolutionary activity. The classic illustration is the Chicxulub meteor strike that killed off the dinosaurs sixty-five million years ago, giving rise to an explosion of new life. Gould and Eldredge posited that dramatic evolutionary shifts aren't due to incremental changes but to these kinds of unforeseen events.

In education, there have been such moments. The printing press was one. It transformed books from the private preserve of monasteries, royal libraries, and the fortunate few into a universal means for sharing knowledge, and literacy from an oddity into a prized skill. For American education, waves of Catholic immigration prompted nineteenth-century Common School reformers' frenzied efforts to remake schooling. In the late 1950s, the launch of *Sputnik* was another such moment, as the Soviet satellite launch fueled an explosion of activity in math and science education.

In the early 2020s, American schooling experienced the most consequential disruption in memory. The COVID-19 pandemic stressed and stretched schooling in unprecedented ways. Routines that had been in place for generations came to a crashing halt. Suddenly, children weren't boarding buses. Some families went a year or more without sending their child to school. Some teachers went a year or more without seeing their students in person. School lunches, field trips, and dances went away. Rhythms that had felt preordained no longer felt quite so certain. In short, the traditions of American education were turned inside out.

SCHOOLS HAVE BEEN UPENDED

Schools are funny places. They're the most human and formative of institutions, with cultures shaped by thousands upon thousands of tiny interactions each day. But the need to manage all that unruliness can also make them among the most bureaucratic and hidebound.

Perhaps this tension is why schools are steadily bombarded by wave upon wave of proposed changes, yielding a culture of "spinning wheels" in which veteran educators wait out each successive wave as they wearily reassure one another "this too shall pass."[12]

As historians David Tyack and Larry Cuban observed many years ago in *Tinkering Toward Utopia*, proposals surface "again and again in cyclical fashion." They wryly offered a partial list, noting that reformers alternately champion things like "student-centered pedagogy or teacher-centered instruction," "attention to academic or to practical knowledge," and "centralized or decentralized governance of schools."[13]

The constant wash of reform makes it tough for any proposal to stick (or even be taken seriously). But there's reason to think that the post-pandemic era could be a moment of "punctuated equilibrium" rather than another spin of the reform wheel.

Shaken by the pandemic, families expressed frustration and an appetite for new options. Given heightened visibility into the classroom, many parents grew increasingly engaged—sometimes to the consternation of teachers or school leaders.[14]

Asked to grade the nation's schools, in 2022, just one in five Americans gave them an A or B.[15] In 2021, 55 percent of parents said American education was "on the wrong track."[16] Also in 2021, 44 percent of the public gave the nation's police a grade of A or B, nearly twice the 23 percent who graded schools the same way (and this was after a year of intense national attention to police misconduct).[17]

Meanwhile, during the pandemic, homeschooling spiked. Tens of thousands of learning pods sprouted across the land. The phenomenon of hybrid homeschools (tiny schools that feature some blend of homeschooling and remote learning) grew into a national network.[18] The pandemic drove enrollment increases at charter and private schools, and historic declines in traditional public schools (especially in the big districts that stayed remote the longest).[19]

The pandemic shattered established relationships, eroded parent trust, and exhausted educators. That adds up to a lot of fertile ground for rethinking.

Exercise 1.1 Check Your Understanding: A Little History Quiz

School rules and routines are so familiar that they can seem immutable. That's a problem. To help kick-start the rethinking process, it's useful to talk a bit about *why* schools look the way they do, about how we got here. This exercise works best in small groups and takes roughly twenty-five minutes.

How It Works

Organize participants into small groups and ask them to discuss and then answer the following questions as best they can (guessing is wholly encouraged; Googling is not). Give the groups about eight to ten minutes to answer the quiz. The questions are:

1. What were the first laws providing for public education in what's now the United States?
2. Back in 1800, what percentage of the nation's teachers were women?
3. What percentage of American eighteen-year-olds were graduating from high school in 1900?
4. Where did the United States rank on international reading and math tests in 1930?
5. In the 1950s, what share of female college graduates went into teaching?
6. What percentage of the nation's schools were connected to the internet in 1990?

After the groups generate their guesses, take another fifteen to twenty minutes as a whole group to discuss the answers, consider what participants did or didn't already know, and reflect on what we should make of all this.

The Answers

1. It's a bit of a trick question (since "now the United States" can be misleading), but the answer is the Old Deluder Satan Acts adopted by Massachusetts Bay Colony in the 1640s. Communities with enough households were required to arrange for schooling so that kids would learn to read the Bible and avoid being ensnared by "the old deluder," Satan.
2. In the colonial era, 90 percent of teachers were men—and teaching was largely short-term, itinerant work that they did for a year or two. That didn't really change until the middle of the nineteenth century, when "Common School" reformers feminized teaching in search of cheaper, more reliable labor.
3. Only about 6 or 7 percent of eighteen-year-olds graduated from high school in 1900. Of course, this was an era when four out of five workers labored on farms or in factories. Today, 85 percent of eighteen-year-olds graduate from high school and just one in five jobs are in agriculture or manufacturing.
4. While one can find internet materials which claim that US schools led the world a century ago, those purported facts are fake. This is a trick question. *There were no international tests in 1930* and no regular attempt at international assessments until the 1990s. There's no evidence that American schools ever fared markedly better than they do today.
5. Over half of college-educated women became teachers in the 1950s, at a time when other professions were mostly closed to them. Today, that captive labor force no longer exists. Yet, school districts still tend to recruit teachers like it's the 1950s, wooing college graduates with the promise of starting a job that they'll be in three decades from now.
6. No schools were linked to the internet in 1990 because the internet, as we know it, didn't yet exist.

Takeaways

The purpose of schooling has shifted profoundly over time (from keeping kids away from Satan to "preparing all students for college or career"). Expectations have changed: high school graduation is no longer a rarity; it's now a baseline. There have been extraordinary shifts in the labor force, the nature of professional work, and the tools that schools have at their disposal. While educators, parents, and community leaders don't usually think much about any of this, it helps explain why taken-for-granted routines may leave schools ill-equipped to do much that they're asked to do today. By illustrating how little we may know about why schools work the way they do, this exercise can shake up comfortable notions of how schooling is supposed to work and leave participants a bit more willing to consider alternatives.

SCHOOLS WEREN'T DESIGNED FOR WHAT THEY'RE ASKED TO DO TODAY

I've found that a lot of listeners nod along when someone says, "American schools weren't designed to do much of what we ask them to do today." But I've also learned that many of those same listeners don't necessarily grasp why that is or why it matters.

Well, it matters because American schooling, as we know it today, is not the product of careful planning or sacred design. There's no obvious reason yesterday's makeshift attendance zones, school calendars, or staffing models should be regarded as the measure of how schools are supposed to work.

In that spirit, I want to take a moment to sketch a thumbnail version of US education history (of how we got here) that can provide a framework for what follows.[20]

Back in the mid-1600s, the Massachusetts Bay Colony adopted the first colonial policies requiring the provision of schools. It then took more than three centuries to build a school system in which 90 percent of America's school-age youth went to school each day. For most of that time we asked schools to focus on molding students into God-fearing citizens, without much concern for academic performance or "postsecondary success."

In the 1830s and 1840s, Massachusetts school board chief Horace Mann launched America's first great experiment in school reform. Mann and his fellow reformers thought that erecting common schools, where all kids would read the King James Bible, would help combat the "threat" to the republic posed by Catholic immigrants from Ireland, Italy, and Eastern Europe. The challenge: Mann's strategy required cheap, plentiful teachers. The solution: turn teaching from a mostly male position into women's work.

As the twentieth century dawned, common schools delivered only a rudimentary education to most children. In 1900, just one out of fifteen eighteen-year-olds completed high school. Those tempted to imagine some kind of idealized education past do well to keep in mind that it's much easier to produce accomplished graduates when just 6 percent of students are earning a diploma. Of course, in that era, farms and factories employed four out of five workers, which meant that schooling was widely (and not unreasonably) viewed as something of a luxury.

In the early twentieth century, Progressive Era reformers set out to universalize education by erecting a host of new schools, organizing them in more systematic ways, and expanding the teacher workforce. Entranced by the promise of "scientific management," Progressive reformers sought to infuse education with the best practices of the era's factories. They embraced top-down management, testing, and standardized record-keeping, confident in the ability of administrators to micromanage ranks of interchangeable teachers.

This approach yielded lots of dubious behavior. Teachers could be fired for getting married, being pregnant, or failing to conform to height and weight charts. In response, (quite understandably!) educators fought for protections like tenure, work rules, and salary schedules. At the time, these wins were a sensible corrective to capricious management. They also meant, though, that public schools would operate under a blanket of increasingly rigid policies governing how staff were hired, how they were evaluated and compensated, and what they did all day. That is still true today.

It was well into the twentieth century before we finally got most of the nation's youth to attend school on a daily basis. Then, pretty quickly, our goals changed. By the 1980s and 1990s, keeping kids off the streets and teaching them to be on time was no longer enough; we wanted schools to prepare every child for the knowledge economy and to be engines of opportunity in a manner that would've been unimaginable even a few decades prior.

These new goals were good and right . . . but, whew! That's quite an order, especially when talking about 14,000 school systems and 100,000 schools designed primarily to fight temptation, promote basic skills, and keep kids occupied. The men and women who built those schools never had reason to wonder: "Will these classrooms, schedules, staffing practices, or school routines help nurture powerful learning for all children in the 2020s?"

If they'd ever dwelled on that, I think there's a pretty good chance they'd have said, "Not our problem. These schools were built for us. *That* job is going to be on you."

WHERE WE GET STUCK

So, we've got a system of schooling that was never designed to do what we're asking it to do. Worse, decades of heralded efforts to reform it have disappointed. Indeed, more than a decade ago, I wrote a book called *The Same Thing Over and Over*, arguing that well-meaning twentieth- and twenty-first-century school reforms frequently foundered because organizational routine, political interests, and inertia all combined stymie them.

Well, as we've noted, events may have conspired to make a more profound shift possible. Embracing that promise, however, requires that we avoid the traps that have hobbled so many previous efforts.

The Innovation Trap

I know it probably seems counterintuitive in a book about "The Great Rethink," but I regard "innovation" as a dirty word. One of the things that's consistently tripped up educational improvement over the years is the cult of innovation and the unhealthy fascination with innovative models.

What's my gripe? Well, innovation isn't actually a thing. Here's what I mean: walk into an Apple store and tell the salesperson you'd like to buy an "innovative" iPhone. Reach out to Tesla and say you want to buy a really "innovative" car. These companies are known as innovators, and yet the staff would look at you like you were a nut. Why? Because innovation isn't a thing—it's a lazy adjective. (This is why you should flee if a salesperson ever tells you, "This gadget is super innovative!" What they're really saying is, "It does lots of useless things in flashy ways!")

Understood rightly, innovation is a means, not an end. It's a process, not a goal. Today's cars are safer than they were twenty years ago. They get more miles to the gallon, and some electric cars can go vast distances on a single charge. Today's iPhones have mind-blowing cameras and processing capacity. They can communicate and monitor health data in ways that would boggle the minds of the engineers who staffed NASA's lunar program. But none of this was due to some vague call to innovate. These changes were attempts to solve practical problems. Now, solving those problems *entailed* innovation, but innovation was the by-product—not the goal.

In other words, what matters is what these things do. Whether they're innovative is irrelevant. *That's* why *innovation* is a bad word. It's a distraction. It gets us focused on the wrong things. It pulls us away from asking whether this change is good for students, educators, or learning, and toward whether it sounds cool.

Don't fall into that trap.

The "Best Practice" Trap

Talk of educational improvement features a *lot* of enthusiastic invocations of "best practices." Best practices are things that supposedly have been proven to work. But there are problems with that notion of "proven."

Consider best practices when it comes to curricular alignment, extended learning time, social and emotional learning (SEL) programs, teacher evaluation models, counselor ratios, or professional development (PD). All these can add value, when done wisely and well. There are studies and analyses that suggest just this. But there is also plenty of research showing disappointing results. And, if you look closely, you'll notice that the most positive studies are conducted in favorable circumstances, frequently by researchers who favor the reform in question.

In other words, "proven" really means that, if you do these things *exactly* the way the research subjects did, for similar students under favorable conditions, there's a good chance they'll help. Unfortunately, the world rarely works that way. It's nearly impossible to exactly duplicate anything, let alone a complex school program or policy. Heck, even high-quality studies rarely explain precisely how an intervention worked or just what's involved.

Thus, when someone claims that something is a best practice, what they usually mean is that they can point to a handful of studies suggesting that it has worked in carefully executed programs under controlled conditions—and, if your school or system does something sort of similar, they think that's recommendation enough.

The result is that programs and practices get adopted and implemented pretty haphazardly. What results is far from a precise imitation of the model, even in those instances when it's clear how the model program worked. And these replications frequently yield disappointing results.

So, best practices usually aren't really best practices at all. It's usually more accurate to say they're "well-meaning notions." The bigger problem is that they offer the false assurance that leaders can deliver hoped-for results if they just adopt the right slate of currently fashionable practices. That has served to discourage attention to more deep-seated changes in how schools think about time, talent, technology, and their relationship with families.

The Dog-and-Pony Trap

Until the late twentieth century, it was not unusual for a community to rely on one local store for many or most of its needs. The Sears, Roebuck and Co. catalog from a century ago featured everything from firearms, baby carriages, and jewelry to saddles and eyeglasses (with a self-test for "old sight, near sight and astigmatism").[21] There was generally a single kind of soap or toothpaste, and customers felt fortunate to get that.

If this all seems hopelessly antiquated today, that's because it is. In a world where we hop online to get what we want from any number of vendors, it's hard to fathom being so constrained. Yet school districts tend to operate as if they're still in the world of country stores and mail-order catalogs. Delivering a new reading program entails sending a handful of staff to visit an acclaimed district for a two-day dog-and-pony show, as if they're checking out a celebrated Sears store in Pittsburgh. The staff then fly home and seek to mimic what they saw, relying on local staff and a bit of overpriced consulting support.

This mindset is a big reason why so many school districts have scrambled to build their own virtual schools from scratch, even though remote schooling can be provided by savvy veterans in Silicon Valley or Seattle (or in Singapore or Senegal) as readily as from downtown. It's as if hundreds or thousands of communities felt a need to erect their own Amazon, Google, or Netflix.

Sure, a given virtual school will need to reflect state standards and incorporate district curricula. But the insistence on district staff constantly recreating the wheel is a recipe for frustration. Rather than virtual schools designed or operated by organizations that serve thousands of schools, districts are launching one more project for overstretched district IT staff and local teachers to bootstrap—at least until a new superintendent arrives with a different program and a new batch of consultants. The intent and effort are admirable; the results less so.

RETHINKING IN THE REAL WORLD

The easiest thing in the world to do is *talk* about improvement. It's vastly tougher to actually do it. But, if you're busy doing it without thinking long and hard about *what* you're doing and *why*, mammoth efforts can yield meager gains. As the British philosopher Bertrand Russell once put it, "In all affairs, it's a healthy thing now and then to hang a question mark on the things you have long taken for granted."

I'll try to put this more plainly. Think of a scrum of little kids building a sandcastle at the ocean's edge. They can shovel, scoop, hustle, and hurry, only to see their project be repeatedly washed away.

Don't get me wrong. Hard work matters. Careful execution matters. Elbow grease matters. But, if we think about that sandcastle, the big problem is that the kids are building it in the wrong spot. If they paused and moved twenty feet up the beach, the *exact same effort* would deliver a much more satisfying result.

Rethinking isn't an alternative to the hard work of improving curriculum, instruction, educator morale, or student well-being. It's a way to facilitate those efforts. Three principles help make this a practical exercise rather than a theoretical one.

Exercise 1.2   Take a Step Back: What Is a "School," Anyway?

Just what is it that makes something a school? Is it the building? The desks? The staffing ratio? This is a useful framing exercise that can help nudge participants to revisit some taken-for-granted assumptions. This exercise works best in small groups and takes about twenty to twenty-five minutes.

How It Works

Ask each group, "What makes something a school?" Give groups ten minutes to write a one-sentence definition and list five elements that make something a school. (Have groups create posters so that participants can see one another's responses.) Then, take about ten to fifteen minutes to have groups share definitions and reflect on what they heard. Definitions frequently tend toward the amorphous (e.g., "school is a place where youth develop as people"). When that happens, respond with queries that mirror the sentiment: "Is a basketball team a school if it's a place where youth develop as people?" Other times, groups will tend toward the uber-literal—saying that schools are places "where teachers teach academic subjects" or "where states require children to go every day." Work to unpack what the declarations mean: "If children were required to report to a factory every day, would that make it a school?" "Can there be schools where students don't go every day or where teachers don't teach academic subjects?"

Takeaways

It's a lot trickier to define a school than it may seem. The dictionary defaults to "an institution for educating children." That's true, of course, but doesn't tell us much of value. It's not clear that schools need to meet for a certain number of hours each week or days each year, cover a particular set of subjects, or organize students into fixed classes or groupings. While we're used to thinking of schools in such terms, it may be that these traits are more familiar than they are fundamental. Schools look like they do because these rhythms and routines once made sense; that doesn't mean they still do. Expectations, student circumstances, and desired outcomes have changed in fundamental ways. Perhaps schooling should, as well.

Retire the One-Stop-Shop Schoolhouse

Once upon a time, communication and transportation imposed harsh limits on schooling. Back in the 1980s (much less the 1880s!) students really needed to be in the same room as a teacher to learn from them. For students to read a book in class, schools needed sets of printed copies. Students could only be mentored or tutored by adults who lived within driving distance and had the time and means to meet them at school or the local library.

Schools operated as buildings that provided a sprawling array of services to students who lived in a geographic area. It made sense, but was also a lot to ask. After all, it's hard for any organization to do many different things, much less do them all well. Advances in technology have made it so that schools no longer need be one-stop shops for everything. It's now possible for students to access books, tutoring, courses, and even telehealth online, creating an extraordinary opening to ask how schools *should* be organized.

Today, school staff have to juggle all manner of tasks. Being a "teacher" means being an evaluator, remediator, lesson designer, hallway monitor, counselor, computer troubleshooter, secretary, coffeemaker, and more. Maybe it doesn't have to be this way. Are there better ways to organize the work that schools and teachers do, so as to empower educators while making their jobs more manageable?

A good way to think about this is as "unbundling," as in whether it's possible to tease apart the many tasks schools have bundled together and then assemble them in more fruitful ways.[22] This means asking what schools and educators should do by themselves, or when and how they might be better off tapping today's vibrant ecosystem of nonschool resources and programs. Instead of lamenting how much schools and teachers are expected to do today, Rethinkers ask what we *should* expect them to do.

Take Personalization Seriously

Education is full of flowery talk about personalization. That's fine. I sure don't know anyone who says, "Schools should be *less personal* and more industrial." In practice, though, school improvement efforts billed as "personalized" can have the opposite effect.

Remember that annual state testing was promoted, in part, as a way to be sure that individual students didn't get overlooked. Yet the biggest complaint about annual assessment may be the way it can turn schools into impersonal test-prep factories. Education technology is touted as a tool of radical personalization. Yet, as we saw during the pandemic, remote instruction and classrooms of tablet-fixated kids can too easily feel dreary and soulless.

Giving students a Chromebook or an iPad is not personalization. The personalization resides in how these tools are used. Think of it this way: fifty years ago, if you wanted to listen to your favorite song, you'd buy a record, go home, put it on your record player, and listen to the album one side at a time. The same applied to every person who wanted to hear that song. Personalizing your music wasn't easy. Digital music technology has changed all that. Today, any listener has easy access to intricate algorithms that pick among millions of songs to create customized playlists that reflect personal preferences.

In education, personalization requires asking how tools and policies can be used to meet the varied needs of every learner. Expanded choices can better allow students at a given school to access courses, instructors, and programs that would otherwise be unavailable. New options may make it possible for bullied students to find a healthier, more welcoming environment or for parents to work more closely with their child on an array of school assignments. New technologies can allow one-size-fits-all curricula to be reconceived as more individualized playlists. But moving any of this from theory to practice is no easy thing.

Know What Problem You're Solving

Education has a "fire, ready, aim" problem. Fueled by the high hopes of advocates and the expectation that every new superintendent will show up with novel solutions, education cycles through scads of reforms at an alarming pace. This makes it tough to be sure that the proposed fix is a good match for the problem—or even that we know exactly what the problem is.

Before leaping on some new program or practice, Rethinkers first seek to define the problem they're trying to solve. Anything else can do more harm than good, with the serial embrace of reflexive solutions turning into a convenient distraction from the real work at hand.

When I talk about distractions, I'm thinking of the district that moved to digital textbooks and a digital curriculum before ensuring that the devices would work as needed. The superintendent got cheered as an innovator, but students and teachers wound up worse off. Books and resources took forever to load, turning ten-minute assignments into marathon sessions. Kids found it tough to do homework on the bus or on the way to soccer since they couldn't get reliable access to online assignments. And that's all separate from the frustrations of teachers who struggled with glitchy portals and forgotten passwords. The heralded "solution" created more problems than it solved.

A new SEL initiative might help if middle schoolers are disengaged, but probably not if their disinterest is due to confusing math instruction. Knowing whether an intervention will help requires knowing what the problem is. Which kids are struggling? Why? How do we know? Be skeptical of those who offer surefire solutions before getting those answers. Programs and policies should be the final step of rethinking, not the first.

Exercise 1.3   Imagine If: The Importance of Crisp Communication

When school leaders, teachers, and parents talk past one another, school improvement becomes a fool's errand. If we can't understand one another, we can't diagnose challenges, explore solutions, or accomplish much of anything. Unfortunately, misunderstandings can be as much a part of the schoolhouse as books and backpacks. This exercise is designed to help participants reflect on the perils of miscommunication and how to avoid it. It works best in pairs and takes about twenty to twenty-five minutes.

How It Works

Pairs should take five minutes to reflect on this charge: "We've all had times when we were misunderstood. Try to recall a time in your professional life or school experience when that happened to you and how it felt." Each member of a pair should share an experience. Next, participants should take five minutes to try and identify some of the circumstances that fueled the misunderstanding. What was the nature of it? Was it due to assumptions? Unclear language? Misaligned expectations? Personal animosity? At this point, the whole group should take ten to fifteen minutes to share some of the misunderstandings, describe the circumstances that contributed, and discuss what might have helped avoid it. A good closing task is for pairs to take a few moments to settle on three practices that can help minimize misunderstanding.

Takeaways

It's frustrating to deal with someone who doesn't understand you. That kind of interaction can leave us hesitant to ask questions or offer suggestions. That's bad for morale and it's death for rethinking. Participants are usually happy to share experiences. The point is to help them ruminate on what makes for clear communication, what gets in the way, and how to be more cognizant of that in the moment. Participants routinely surface important considerations relating to bias and culture, but it's good to make sure the discussion also touches on the value of conveying essential information, avoiding superfluous trivia, and speaking in ways that resonate with the listener.

HOW TO BE A "RETHINKER"

A Rethinker knows schools can do much better but is dubious of surefire, one-size-fits-all solutions. A Rethinker is open to reimagining how schools use time, talent, money, and engage with families, and believes that such a project is wholly compatible with a commitment to public education. Given that, there are five habits that a Rethinker takes to heart.

> *Ask why . . . a lot!* The best way to resist the temptation to attack poorly understood problems with half-baked fixes is simply by asking "Why?" as in, "Why is this person doing this task?" or, "Why do we give that activity that much time?" Asking questions creates an opportunity to pause and reflect, one that is almost invariably more valuable than a well-practiced answer. It's not enough to ask the questions, though. It's critical that Rethinkers also encourage *others* to ask them and that they foster a culture where asking "why?" is expected (and valued).

This means discouraging hurried fixes and creating opportunities for inconvenient questions.

Be precise. Years ago, in *Cage-Busting Leadership*, I shared an example of how imprecise thinking can stymie school and system leaders. I'd been digging into a big district's efforts to stop routinely granting tenure to mediocre teachers. As I noted: "There was much talk about better recruiting and improved evaluation. Yet, it soon became clear that a key reason no one was denied tenure was that the system *had never bothered to generate the forms required to terminate a probationary teacher*." You need to know what the problem is in order to solve it. The lesson is simple: precision counts.[23]

Take a deep breath. Education is filled with passionate people. That's a good thing. But it also means school improvement gets tackled by those who are sure they know what needs to be done and are in a hurry to do it. One consequence is a tendency to vilify those who aren't on board with the reform du jour (if I'm "for the kids" and you're not with me, you must be anti-kid). Another is planning that tends toward the haphazard and imprecise (if we know what to do and we're in a hurry, it doesn't matter if our plan amounts to little more than a mess of jargon on a cut-and-paste PowerPoint). Intent on appreciating how changes will actually work, a Rethinker knows the value of taking a deep breath and then moving deliberately.

Know that new problems may call for new solutions. When problems change, the answers can too. This isn't rocket science. In 1900, when four out of five jobs resided on a farm or in a factory, an academic education just wasn't that important. In our twenty-first-century economy, it's crucial. A hundred years ago, there was no simple way to travel across the country, track lots of information, or casually talk to experts around the globe. Today, all of that is possible—even convenient. And, as things change, new needs, challenges, and solutions emerge. A Rethinker accepts that. It isn't about romanticizing the new but acknowledging that there are times when it makes sense to overhaul comfortable routines or reimagine familiar institutions.

Reject change for change's sake. G. K. Chesterton famously suggested that we ought not "reform" things until we understand them. In his 1929 book *The Thing*, Chesterton wrote, "[Imagine] a fence or gate erected across a road. The more modern type of reformer goes gaily up to it and says, 'I don't see the use of this; let us clear it away.' To which the more intelligent type of reformer will do well to answer: 'If you don't see the use of it, I certainly won't let you clear it away.'" Chesterton's point was that removing the fence without knowing if, say, it still keeps cows from wandering into a road could be dangerous (for cattle and drivers alike). In judging the merits of change, we should always keep in mind Chesterton's caution.[24]

THE BOOK AHEAD

"What are you doing differently today than you did three years ago?" It's a question that Louisiana state superintendent Cade Brumley likes to ask his principals, and it's a good one. It invites school leaders to reflect on what they're doing, how it's changed, and why. In my experience, that's something we all do too rarely in education.

I think of the associate superintendent who told me, "In a system like ours, we're running flat-out from sunrise to sunset. It's tough to do too much of what you're talking about when we're busy putting out fires all day."

It's a fair point. Leaders spend a lot of time scrambling. That can mean they spend more time reacting than rethinking. That focus also means that the reform mantle often winds up being worn by advocates, funders, pundits, and public officials who don't have to make the reforms work. I think that goes a long way to explaining the shape of education today.

Foundation honchos and TED talkers love issuing high-minded calls to "reset education for the twenty-first century." Pretty much every US Secretary of Education this century, for instance, has called for "transformational" change and then oversold a smorgasbord of not-so-transformative policies like testing, school improvement planning, test-based teacher evaluation, reading and math standards, or expanded school choice.

Some of these proposals were sensible, some less so. But none of them were all that likely to transform what schools and teachers do. Worse, the mismatch between grand talk and modest change fuels cynicism. Indeed, the foundation officials, advocates, and politicos who talk of transformation tend to be the furthest removed from having to do any of it. Meanwhile, those most affected by it—like educators and parents—are the most skeptical of it.

That should tell us something. While it's easy to imagine that rethinking starts with big talk of sweeping transformation, it doesn't. It starts by focusing on what's not working for students, families, and educators and asking how to address the challenges. After that, everything else is details.

Now, before we proceed, there's one potential distraction I should address. My experience is that some readers may mistakenly construe much of what I've said here as an "attack" on public education (or even on teachers). I think that has it exactly backward. I see rethinking as profoundly pro-teacher. Just as students and parents may feel stymied by their schools and school systems, the same holds for plenty of educators. The routines and assumptions that can infuriate families also frustrate the teachers who live them every day. Rethinking seeks to be both implacably pro-student and profoundly pro-educator.

And if rethinking is pro-teacher, the same applies tenfold when it comes to public education's broader promise. Ensuring that schools equip every child for life success and citizenship should *require* regularly asking whether there are better ways to keep that promise. If old rules or routines are getting in the way, rethinking is not just appropriate—it's obligatory.

Anyway, that's how I see things.

Now, as for what's ahead. In the next chapter, we'll turn to how schools use time. In chapter 3, we'll examine how they use talent. In chapter 4, we'll take up the challenge of education technology. In chapter 5, we'll see if we can do a little rethinking on the issue of school choice. In chapter 6, we'll try to take a fresh look at the parent-school relationship. And, in chapter 7, we'll talk about how all of this fits with the public school tradition and how to start putting theory into practice.

With that, let's begin.

CHAPTER 2

What We Do with Time

The pandemic shed a harsh light on what schools do with time. When school leaders across the land abruptly concluded they could squeeze a seven-hour school day into three hours of remote teaching (or fifty-five minutes of asynchronous instruction), it raised hard questions about what students do all day. When push came to shove, the traditional school day no longer seemed sacrosanct.

Back in 1994, the National Education Commission on Time and Learning observed, "Learning in America is a prisoner of time. For the past 150 years, American public schools have held time constant and let learning vary. The rule, only rarely voiced, is simple: learn what you can in the time we make available."[1]

Given the conviction that learning is limited by the available time, it's no surprise that one evergreen proposal is for kids to spend more time in school. In summer 2022, nearly half of school districts used emergency pandemic-related federal funds to offer summer instruction. A third of districts said they were using those funds to add time to the school day.[2]

And yet the "more time" solution is ultimately unsatisfying because too many schools are cavalier when it comes to how they use the time they already have. If "extended learning time" means locking kids in a building for paper-shuffling or soporific instruction, it hardly seems like an improvement. Allison Socol, an analyst at the Education Trust, has put it more diplomatically, observing, "Just adding extra minutes onto the day in and of itself isn't necessarily going to help students make learning gains."[3]

And before we start adding time, there are many ways to make better use of existing student and staff time. This is a key element in some of the approaches popularized by Doug Lemov in his influential book *Teach Like a Champion*. As Lemov pointed out:

> Assume that the average class of students passes out or back papers and materials twenty times a day and that it takes a typical class a minute and twenty seconds to do this. If . . . students can accomplish this task in just twenty seconds, they will save twenty minutes a day (one minute each time) . . . Now multiply that twenty minutes per day by 190 school days, and you find that [the time saved is] thirty-eight hundred minutes of additional instruction over the course of a school year. That's more than sixty-three hours or almost eight additional days of instruction.[4]

Or consider the experience of the 1,000-student middle school that was getting 200 parental notifications a day regarding tardy arrivals, early pickups, and such. Each call or note took a minute or two of staff time, totaling something like 200 to 400 minutes a day (or 15 to 35 hours a week). That equates to perhaps 600 to 1,200 hours of staff time during a school year. By adopting a mobile interface that instantly tagged relevant staff, red-flagged any problems, and spit out an official record, the school recaptured a big chunk of time—even as it simplified record-keeping and reduced miscommunication.

While such a tool has obvious limits, it means that the run-of-the-mill stuff is no longer a steady drain on staff time, attention, and energy. It allows hundreds of hours to be redirected to instructional coaching, mentoring, parent outreach, and the like.

It's easy to take time for granted. But most of what schools do is buy time. Close to 80 percent of school spending is for salary and benefits, all of it spent to pay for people's time. As Lemov puts it, "[Time] is a teacher's most precious resource—it is to be husbanded, guarded, and preserved. Every minute of it matters, and the way we use it shows students where our priorities are."[5]

So, yeah, time matters.

HOW A PENSION FUND CAME TO DICTATE THE HIGH SCHOOL SCHEDULE

The very rhythm of schooling is driven by the use and measure of time, from master schedules to required hours of instruction. State laws are dotted with requirements governing seat time hours and minutes per day.[6] While these arrangements may have once made good sense, they shape schooling today in ways that don't always obviously promote teaching or learning.

For a telling example, one need look no further than the Carnegie Unit—the ubiquitous, if far-from-beloved, standard measure of high school course credit. How did high school scheduling, course-taking, and curricula come to be so thoroughly shaped by the Carnegie Unit? Hint: it wasn't about pedagogy.

In 1905, steel baron Andrew Carnegie told college presidents he wanted to establish a pension system for college professors (because he regarded theirs as "one of the poorest paid but highest professions in our nation"). Carnegie, then the world's richest man, created the Carnegie Foundation for the Advancement of Teaching to run the system. He gave it $10 million to get started. At the time, though, higher education was something of a Wild West, and it wasn't even clear which institutions should qualify as "colleges" for his new pension system.[7]

Well, Carnegie's foundation decided that one way colleges could prove they were "real" colleges was by requiring students to have at least four years of high school preparation. At a time when not even 10 percent of eighteen-year-olds earned a high school diploma, and when the nature of schooling varied wildly from place to place, it was tricky to measure if students had completed four years of high school. The foundation developed the Carnegie Unit in 1906 in order to solve that problem.

To earn one unit of high school credit, students needed 120 hours of study in a given subject (or a bit over three hours of class time a week during a thirty-six-week school year). Thus, the Carnegie Unit was born. Fourteen of these units were judged to constitute four years of high school.

In time, this measure designed to help a steel magnate establish pensions for college professors became an indelible part of K–12 schooling.[8] Whatever one thinks of the Carnegie Unit as a solution to the educational challenges of 1905 (it strikes me as a fairly reasonable one), it doesn't seem like an especially useful way to gauge learning today. As historians David Tyack and Larry Cuban observed in *Tinkering Toward Utopia*, critics have argued that the Carnegie Unit has "frozen schedules, separated knowledge into discrete boxes, and created an accounting mentality better suited to a bank than to a school."[9] That sounds about right.

THE SCHOOL CALENDAR IS FROZEN IN TIME

It's not just the Carnegie Unit that has locked schools into the trappings of an earlier era. It's often noted that the American school calendar is an anachronism geared for the needs of nineteenth-century farmers—rather than twenty-first-century learners. That's half right.

The school calendar is an anachronism. But that's not because it was designed for farmers, who tend to be busiest in the spring and fall (during planting and harvesting season) when school is in session. Indeed, in many nineteenth-century rural communities, schooling was haphazard, with schools open just three to six months a year.[10]

Instead, the adoption of the summer break was a response to urban challenges of the late 1800s. Health authorities regarded sweltering cities, with raw sewage running in the gutters (back before air-conditioning or modern plumbing), as a breeding ground for disease. The goal was to enable families to get children out of crowded, dirty cities in the summer heat while addressing concerns that too much schooling would overtax students.[11]

Over time, public hygiene evolved, but the school calendar did not. A one-size-fits-all summer break became entrenched in a nation where students and families come in many sizes and with many different needs. Long summers work well for some families, especially those of means, with adequate childcare, and in which parents have flexible jobs. Such families find much value in a summer break that allows for camps, travel, and family time. And that's a good thing.

But there are also many families for whom the traditional summer is a poor fit. For families that lack resources, have no parent at home during the day, or live in chaotic or unsafe neighborhoods, summer can be a time when kids are adrift, vulnerable, and restless. "Summer learning loss" explains much of the gap in academic achievement between students from low-income and high-income households, since more affluent students have more access to stimulating camps and cool vacations than their peers. All of this means that summer schooling—*if* it's active, invigorating, and professional—can be a practical and appealing solution for many families. Especially given concerns that too many unattended kids will otherwise spend long days gaming, watching videos, or cruising iffy websites, it's easy to understand why many parents want access to structured, supervised activities.

So, what's the point? It's not, "Ah-ha! This is why we need an extended school year, or year-round schooling." Rather, it's that a century-old schedule shaped by nineteenth-century hygiene concerns may not be a particularly good fit for many students, families, and communities today. That argues for rethinking the options, swapping yesterday's one-size-fits-all model out for a new one.

Exercise 2.1   Imagine If: Rethinking the School Year

We're so used to the rhythms of the school day, week, and year that it can be surprisingly hard to focus on what *specific* changes we'd like to see (aside from things like "more instructional time"). This exercise seeks to spark a more concrete conversation. This exercise works well in small groups or pairs and takes twenty to twenty-five minutes.

How It Works

Small groups assume the role of a task force charged by the district with devising a calendar for a new high school. The school system has received a state waiver from all the normal requirements regarding days of attendance, seat time, instructional hours, or anything else. Given this, what would a school day look like? The school week? The year? Should the school employ a uniform calendar for all students or provide families with a menu of options? The discussions generally don't get very far, because the questions are so amorphous that it can be tough to get one's arms around them. So, after ten minutes of initial thoughts, interject the following prompts to make things more concrete:

- How many hours of instructional time do students need? For reading? For math? For the arts?
- How much variability should there be in scheduling from student to student?
- Do all students (and families) need the option of a typical in-school day?
- Should asynchronous days, remote learning, or some kind of home-based time be incorporated as a regular feature?
- How much vacation do students need and what kind of vacation blocks make the most sense?

Give participants fifteen minutes to discuss these prompts. Then return to the first (very broad) charge and try to devise an answer based on the more particular responses.

Takeaways

The goal is to make discussion about the school day and school year more concrete, with less focus on adding time and more on how time is organized. This exercise can also illustrate how a "blue sky" abstract approach to rethinking is frequently less useful than one that starts with a clearer focus on problems and practical alternatives. The answers we get are a product of the questions we ask, which is why asking the right questions matters so much.

HOW MUCH TIME DO KIDS SPEND IN SCHOOL ANYWAY?

You've probably heard advocates or public officials insist that American kids need more time in school. They fret that American kids are getting less instruction than their global peers, and that we need longer school years or days to catch up. As one US Secretary of Education told a congressional hearing a number of years ago, "Our students today are competing against children in India and China. Those students are going to school 25 to 30 percent longer than we are. Our students, I think, are at a competitive disadvantage."[12]

So, should rethinking time start by having students spend more time in school? Not necessarily. For starters, the facts underlying those claims are a bit muddled. Indeed, if we take the data at face value, it turns out that American kids, relatively speaking, spend *a lot* of time in school.

On the one hand, the US school year is on the shorter side when compared to other advanced economies. Most US students attend school 180 days a year.[13] In Finland, the maximum year is 190 days (though many schools employ a shorter calendar).[14] The school year is 190 days in Hong Kong, Germany, and New Zealand; 200 in the Netherlands; 210 in Japan; and 220 in South Korea.[15]

When tallying instructional time, though, it's not just the number of days students attend school; it's also the time in each school day. When that's included, it turns out that American students get at least as much formal schooling as their global peers. The Organisation for Economic Co-operation and Development (OECD) reports that, on average, US students attend school for 8,903 hours over their first nine years in school—which is 1,264 hours *more* than the OECD average.[16] (The typical school day for American students is over six and a half hours. For Finnish students, it's about five hours. In Germany, it's five and a half. In Japan, it's six.[17])

Also, when we think about how much time schools should demand of kids, keep in mind that these tallies don't include the time students spend in transit. While one can debate whether transit should count as "school time," it's surely not personal time. On average, US students spend more than thirty minutes in transit each day. That's two to three hours a week, or ninety hours a year.[18] For students who ride a school bus, average travel time is about 50 minutes a day, or *150 hours a year*.[19]

The point isn't that American students necessarily get enough schooling. After all, if kids spend this much time in school and we're still disappointed with the results, some kind of change may be in order. The point, rather, is that knowing how much time kids spend in school is more complicated than it may initially appear and, *more importantly*, that simply boosting the number of hours or days that kids sit in school may be the wrong goal.

A Rethinker regards a fixation on adding time as misguided and sees value in focusing instead on murkier but more useful questions: How much time is spent in classes? How much of that time is wasted? How much time are students actually engaged in learning? Do students have enough time to master crucial skills and knowledge? And just what does it mean to be "in school," anyway? (Are students "in school" when they're logged into a remote classroom? How about if they've logged in but they're muted, their camera is off, and they're scrolling through videos on their phone?)

WHERE DOES THE TIME GO?

If students spend more time in school than one might guess, why does it feel like there's never enough time? Well, let's start by noting a few big places where time gets lost.

Structural Factors

While it's tough to know how much of kids' time in school is spent actually learning, we can get a sense of how much time is definitely *not*. One telling study sought to figure out what cuts into all that time that the OECD estimates American kids spend in school.[20]

The researchers took a high school in Holyoke, Massachusetts, with 180 days in its academic calendar and started ticking off lost time. There were seven early-release days for PD (with class periods compressed by fourteen minutes), eight days for exams (four at the end of each semester), and another seven mornings set aside for the Massachusetts state test (all classes were paused on these mornings even though only tenth graders took the state exam).

When all was said and done, the analysts estimated that total instructional time in this school during a given year added up to just 62 percent of the 1,076 hours estimated by OECD. That means there were 410 hours devoted to stuff other than instruction.[21] Policies, practices, and programming have a massive impact on how much school time kids spend learning—regardless of the formal length of the school day or year.

Behavioral Norms

In 2021, in a far-too-unusual study of Providence, Rhode Island, researchers Matt Kraft and Manuel Monti-Nussbaum documented just how many disruptions there are in the course of a school day. They estimated that a typical classroom in a Providence public school is interrupted over 2,000 times per year and that these interruptions combine to consume ten to twenty days of instructional time.[22]

Major disruptions included intercom announcements, staff visits, and students entering (or reentering) class in disruptive ways. In explaining the impact of tardiness, for instance, the researchers observed that "[i]n many classrooms, locked doors required late and returning students to knock and a teacher or student to stop what they were doing and open the door. Late students often resulted in taking the teacher away from whole-class instruction to orient the student to the current task."[23]

Kraft and Monti-Nussbaum noted that more than half of the interruptions they observed led to spillover disruptions that amplified the impact. Meanwhile, they found that administrators appeared to greatly underestimate the frequency of these interruptions and the time they consume.[24]

Operational Routines

Several years ago, Nevada's lawmakers enacted a Nevada Educator Performance Framework that required a series of classroom observations and debriefs. So far, so good. Most school leaders find value in such practices. But lawmakers wanted assurance of universal compliance.

The result? A mandatory, summative sixteen-plus-page evaluation for every single teacher, with dozens of indicators that each required multiple "pieces of evidence." School leaders were spending a bit more than three hours writing each teacher's summative evaluation (beyond the observation, note-taking, and debrief time). As one principal asked: "If you have already gone through the standards and observations, the final document is meaningless . . . so why are we spending three hours writing it up?"[25]

One administrator sighed, "I had 567 pages of evaluations on 31 teachers I evaluated," adding, "We have to initial every single page, and have teachers do the same." An internal analysis calculated that principals were spending 150 hours each—or nineteen eight-hour workdays every year—on paperwork that rehashed things they'd already observed, recorded, and discussed with teachers.[26] Bureaucratic requirements and rigid routines can consume big chunks of time that could otherwise be spent supporting or instructing students.

Exercise 2.2   Check Your Understanding: Tackling Lost Learning Time

The school day features a lot of learning time lost to unintended interruptions. Now, it's one thing for kids to spend time running around a playground or bantering with friends (in sensible proportions, that's the kind of "lost" time most educators don't mind). It's another thing, entirely, to expect students to sit in stuffy classrooms listening to announcements drone on or watch disruptions play out. This exercise helps participants identify sources of disruption and think about how to address them. It works best with small groups and takes twenty to thirty minutes.

How It Works

Groups should take five to ten minutes to list at least a half-dozen sources of interruption and guess the amount of time lost to each in a week. The facilitator should then show the research slide (see figure 2.1), summarizing research by

FIGURE 2.1   Types of classroom interruptions

6 Most Significant Interruptions

- Call to classroom phone
- Returning student
- Visit by teacher, staff, or admin
- Tardy student
- Visit by non-classroom student
- Intercom announcement

Other Types of Interruptions

- Fire/intruder drills
- Special assemblies
- Early student pickups
- Student pullouts for sports or clubs
- Janitorial disruptions
- Street/traffic noise
- Classroom volunteers/teacher aids
- Hallway fights
- Make-up tests
- Administrator walkthroughs
- Extra students added to classes due to a lack of substitutes
- Ambulance/police sirens
- Technology and computer cart issues

Source: Matthew A. Kraft and Manuel Monti-Nussbaum, "The Big Problem with Little Interruptions to Classroom Learning," *AERA Open 7,* no. 1 (2021): 9, 13, doi:10.1177/23328584211028856.

Matt Kraft and Manuel Monti-Nussbaum. Each group should be given twenty minutes to choose three types of disruptions (either from their own list and/ or the slide) and discuss ways in which school leaders or individual teachers could reduce their frequency and impact. Groups should then estimate the potential time savings in a year.

Takeaways

Small, taken-for-granted interruptions can have a big cumulative impact. This means that identifying and addressing even seemingly minor disruptions can have substantial benefits. This exercise can also help illustrate how taking the time to focus on specific, seemingly small headaches can surface practical solutions or promising strategies.

THE TIME DIARY APPROACH

So, we know that only 60 percent or so of a school day is used for instruction. Some of the remainder is consumed by distractions and paperwork. But what about the rest of the time? Where does it go? What exactly are students doing all day?

Well, back in 2003, researchers at Columbia University and the University of Maryland published an invaluable study examining how elementary students actually spent their school day. It's a study I'd expect to see repeated dozens of times a year. Bizarrely, it isn't.

The researchers sent a questionnaire, time diary, and parent sign-off form to the teacher of each of the 553 elementary school students in their sample. On a randomly selected school day, teachers filled out time diaries documenting how students spent their time that day. Teachers tracked when each activity began, when it ended, and what the student did during it.[27]

The researchers grouped activities into four categories: academic, enrichment, recess, and maintenance. "Academic" included time devoted to content-based subjects, tasks like homework review and testing, library and study time, field trips, and games that reinforced academic skills. "Enrichment" included curricular offerings that weren't part of the traditional academic curriculum, like physical education, art, music, or health. "Recess" included playtime, hanging out, and breaks. And "maintenance" included other nonlearning activities like homeroom, announcements, meals, bathroom breaks, lining up, cleaning up, fire drills, or packing and unpacking backpacks.

The average elementary student's school day spanned six hours and thirty-five minutes, of which 64 percent was devoted to academic subject activities. Of the remainder, maintenance activities took up 15 percent, enrichment 12 percent, and recess 7 percent.

Notably, the share of the school day devoted to academics shrunk as the school day got longer. The researchers found that students with a seven-hour day wound up with just twenty-nine minutes more academic time than those with a six-hour day. *In short, less than half of the added hour was devoted to academic instruction.*

It's easy to fall into the habit of treating "more school time" as a short-hand for "more learning." That happens all the time when public officials talk about lengthening the school year or school day. But the truth is that a given hour of schooling can yield a lot of learning—or none at all. There's no assurance it will be devoted to boosting academic instruction, or even used productively. When contemplating the time kids spend in school, Rethinkers focus not just on the amount of time but on *how that time is used.*

In some ways, this is another facet of a much-noted pandemic phenomenon, when remote instruction (and especially asynchronous instruction) frequently proved to be a phantasm. For many students, the reported amount of remote instruction bore little relation to how much time they actually spent learning. What matters, of course, is the harder-to-measure learning time, not the easier-to-measure instructional time.

Exercise 2.3   Take a Step Back: Keeping a Time Diary

This can be one of the more labor-intensive exercises in this book, but I've found it worth the effort. The goal is to explore how much time educators spend on an array of tasks, especially those that aren't really related to teaching and learning, and also how their instructional time gets utilized. School staff members (ideally in pairs) should conduct this activity over the course of a school day.

How It Works

Participants should keep a time diary for one full day. This entails recording everything that happens during the day, including prep time, what they do between classes, and in-class activity. Since it can be tricky for teachers to track themselves during class, it's useful for pairs to be organized so that partners will be able to observe each other with a stopwatch and a tracking sheet. (Obviously, practical constraints limit how much of this kind of observation is possible. Participants should accept that and just do the best they can.) It's important that the tracking be simple, straightforward, and comparable. I recommend using the following three-column template, with one column measuring how many minutes were devoted to an activity; one describing the activity in one to two words; and one categorizing the activity as academic, enrichment, recess, or maintenance.

So, the template would look like this:

Time (in minutes)	Activity (description)	Category
4 min.	taking attendance	maintenance
6 min.	morning announcements	maintenance
20 min.	review problems	academic
4 min.	passing worksheets	maintenance
10 min.	class discussion	academic
6 min.	change classes	recess

Takeaways

In my experience, educators tend to assume they already have a good sense of how they're using their time. But that can be because interruptions, distractions, and dead time are so familiar that they roll by unnoticed. When they've completed this exercise, teachers and school leaders are often surprised by how much (or how little) time they actually devoted to a whole range of activities. Giving educators the opportunity to see their day laid out like this can spark unexpected insights and prompt rich conversation about where time is going and what ought to change.

DISENGAGED TIME IS LOST TIME, TOO

Information on what students do during the average school day can be eye-opening, but it can't tell us whether those students are actually engaged. That's a problem because tuned-out students aren't learning—whether or not they're sitting in classrooms and regardless of what they're *supposed* to be doing.

As it turns out, a lot of students spend a lot of school time feeling bored and disengaged. It's enough to raise the question whether students should perhaps spend *less* time in classrooms.

The High School Survey of Student Engagement reports that four out of five public high school students say they're sometimes bored in class, and half say they're often bored.[28] While this survey is dated, having not been administered since 2016, more recent sources echo those findings.[29] The pandemic only made things worse, with nine out of ten teachers saying students were less motivated than before.[30]

And students say they're less engaged as they get older. In 2017, Youth-Truth reported responses from more than 200,000 students: three-quarters of elementary students said they were engaged in school; the number fell to 60 percent among high schoolers.[31] A Gallup study of 500,000 students found that four in five elementary students said they were engaged in school, but that the ratio fell to three in five middle schoolers and just two in five high schoolers.[32]

Think about it this way: if students are engaged 60 percent of the time, a thirty-hour instructional week amounts to more like eighteen hours of actual learning. This means that a 1,080-hour school year amounts to a 650-hour school year. In short, boosting engagement could potentially dwarf the benefits of a longer school day or year. Heck, this means that *less school time could conceivably yield more actual learning time*—if less time in class meant students were more engaged during class.

Exercise 2.4   Imagine If: Gauging Student Engagement

When we talk about "student engagement," it can be unclear just what we mean or how we know when students are disengaged. This exercise is intended to help participants think more critically on this score. It works best in small groups and takes about thirty to thirty-five minutes.

How It Works

Break participants into small groups and give each the following charge: imagine you've been tasked by your school board with gauging student engagement in your school (or system). How would you do that? Give the groups five minutes to discuss. The first impulse is usually to suggest surveys. That's fine but it's rarely clear how those will provide much insight into *when* and *why* students are engaged. So, give the groups another ten minutes to consider additional tools they might use (like observation, focus groups, or diaries) and what they could learn from them. Take a few minutes to discuss, and then tell the groups they've received a $5,000 grant to collect this information as part of an engagement initiative. Give them ten minutes to discuss how they'd spend it to support the strategies they've surfaced.

Takeaways

Talk of "engagement" is often frustratingly vague. Just because students say they're sometimes "disengaged" on a survey doesn't tell us much about what they're feeling or why they feel that way. This suggests the value of thinking more systematically about how educators can better use observation, focus groups, specific survey queries, and diary feedback. This exercise can also help emphasize the importance of diagnosing problems before embracing solutions, as a given strategy (no matter how popular) may be a poor fit for the particular challenges at hand.

A NEW (SCHOOL) DAY

Across most of the land, five days a week, kids wake up a bit after (or before) sunrise and make their way to school. They're there for seven hours or so and then they reverse the trip. This rhythm has been with us for generations, becoming a comfortable norm in the course of the twentieth century—an era when it was assumed that families had limited options, a mom would be home when kids got off the bus, and learning only happened in school.

Those assumptions no longer reflect the world we live in. Thus, we now have fierce fights over start times. Parents have to scramble for afterschool care or worry about latchkey kids because, in many households, no one is home at 3 p.m. We have created no-win scenarios for teens who supervise younger siblings or work to help support their family.

It doesn't have to be this way. Do all students really need to go to school five days a week? Can they use remote options to craft arrangements that are a better fit for their needs? Given that some students love being in classrooms and others don't, can schools give students more say over how much time they spend in school?

We'll talk about this more in chapter 5; for now, just note that such questions surface new possibilities when it comes to school models. Some models might include students working from home one day a week, leaving campus for asynchronous learning after lunch, or providing an 8 a.m.-to-6 p.m. wraparound for families who need it. More options, of course, can mean logistical challenges related to things like contract hours, bus fleets, and legal liability.

That's why Rethinkers are less interested in sweeping proclamations than in asking the right questions, surfacing practical solutions, and moving forward one step at a time.

A FOCUS ON LEARNING RATHER THAN TIME

As any school leader can tell you, the trouble with critiquing school calendars, schedules, and the like is that schools need *some* kind of system when it comes to serving hundreds or thousands of kids. After all, hardly anyone thinks the off-the-clock pandemic experiment was a successful one. When we ditched calendars and bell schedules, a lot of kids got lost and a lot of learning didn't happen.

In other words, while time may be an imperfect measure, we need some way to organize schooling. If not time, then what?

The obvious answer, of course, is "learning." If you've spent much time at education conferences, you've likely heard the mantra again and again: "Instead of time being the constant and learning the variable, make learning the constant and time the variable."

This intuition has fueled promising ideas like "competency-based education," which seeks to replace time-based measurements of learning (like the Carnegie Unit) with ones based on student mastery of skills and knowledge. In some competency-based programs, mastery is tracked via digital "badges," which students accumulate as they progress. In others, demonstrating competency just means that students move to the next level in a class or program. In either case, the trick is identifying key skills and knowledge and then knowing how to accurately measure mastery of them.

That's no picnic. The challenge may be less daunting in some fields, like math or welding, where the scope and sequence are more clearly defined. At other times, as in literature or civics, the work of defining essential competencies is more intimidating. That's a big reason why, so far, efforts to develop digital badges for technical skills have outpaced those for academic K–12 subjects.[33]

For those unfamiliar with how this works: badges frequently take the form of digital icons, which include details such as when the badge was earned, what it entailed, who issued it, and when it expires. After students earn a badge by completing an appropriate online course or task (typically on a platform like Mozilla Open Badges, Credly, Accredible, or Badgr), they can exhibit it on their résumé and on various virtual platforms.[34]

Now, there's no obvious reason any of this *has* to be digital. The Boy Scouts and Girl Scouts were using badges long before the advent of the personal computer. Similarly, a teacher might conceivably track the requisite information on a classroom whiteboard. The problem is that the burdens of assessing mastery and then managing dozens or hundreds of badges would quickly get overwhelming. So, while there's nothing innately digital about all of this, digital tools help make it feasible to assess, track, and share badges on a broad scale.

Thus far, when it comes to K–12 schooling, badging is mostly just an interesting idea. Some school districts, like Los Angeles, have dabbled with digital badges (though it's mostly been for stuff like summer programs).[35] The practical challenge is that, even if they wish to, school systems can't commit to a competency-based model until there are reliable, precise assessments and badges for the relevant skills and knowledge.

It's a bit of a chicken-and-egg dilemma. Absent robust competency-based alternatives, it's tough to move on from time-based policies, but absent a change in those policies, there's only so much room for competency-based schooling.

It's a good reminder that rethinking is always a dance between the practical and the pedagogically promising.

RETHINKING TIME

In his book *Walden*, Henry David Thoreau famously observed, "The cost of a thing is the amount of what I will call life which is required to be exchanged for it."[36] As Harvard University's Arthur Brooks has explained:

> Thoreau's point is not that we should be all work and no play—he was one of history's most prominent critics of that way of living. Rather, he argued that we waste too much of our lives on things we don't value. Without

thinking about it, we are spectacularly failing some cosmic cost-benefit test, as measured not in money but in what matters most: time.[37]

When it comes to how schools use time, many parents and educators can recall some school leader who squeezed out recess or music to add more test prep—and they (justifiably) fear that talk of "rethinking time" is code for that kind of perverse management. Let me be as clear as I can: that is the very antithesis of rethinking time. It gets things *exactly* backward.

The point is not to reduce active, engaged learning in the name of some false "efficiency," but to have kids spend less time as joyless zombies staring at screens or counting down minutes to dismissal.

The goal is to reduce frustrating, unproductive time and increase the amount of time that's devoted to activities which are valuable and rewarding. And, crucially, what should be understood as productive or unproductive may vary from school to school and system to system, meaning it's something that local leaders need to examine and explore.

In *Deep Work*, Cal Newport sketches a productivity strategy called "time blocking," which involves figuring out how to better use time and then scheduling accordingly.[38] It's a good metaphor for rethinking time. In a given school, it may make sense to devote more or less time to academics or the arts; to have students in a building fewer days a week, or more days each year. The answers will vary. But those answers should be purposeful and determined by what students and educators need.

CHAPTER 3

Teaching Reconceived

While it's often said that this teacher is "effective" or that one "ineffective," I'm not sure we know what we really mean by that. During the pandemic, for instance, I heard a *lot* of highly regarded teachers saying that they were having trouble adjusting to online teaching—that their repertoire wasn't designed for pixel-based instruction. I could relate. I was teaching college classes online and found that lessons which had long felt polished suddenly seemed stilted. I felt like a novice as I scrambled to use breakout rooms, share my screen, police background noise, and all the rest.

At the same time, plenty of school leaders remarked that they were pleasantly surprised to find that teachers who'd sometimes struggled in classrooms were surprisingly adept when online. Why would that be? At first, it doesn't make much sense. If some strong teachers were struggling, why would other teachers do better than expected?

It's a good question, but one that pretty much answers itself. Teachers do many different things: They mentor. They encourage. They create lesson plans. They deliver instruction. They troubleshoot balky technology. They discipline unruly kids. When we say a teacher is "effective," do we mean they're good at all those things? Some of them? Which ones?

Some in-person skills translate to remote learning, but not all of them. And remote learning may utilize skills that don't count for as much in person. This can all get pretty complicated. But one simple takeaway is that it's nuts to solely think of teachers as either "good" or "not good." If teachers have both strengths and weaknesses, the challenge is to staff schools in ways that more fully tap their strengths and minimize their weaknesses.

When the pandemic-driven shift to remote learning slashed the amount of teacher-student interaction, it brought home the importance of distinguishing high-value from low-value work. If teachers only have limited time in classrooms (or online), then that time needs to be devoted to things where face-to-face intimacy really matters.

Face-to-face interactions are more important for some instructional tasks than for others. For instance, in a given English language arts classroom, there are skills to build, books to read, concepts to master, content to absorb, essays to write, discussions to hold, reading strategies to learn, and much more. Some of this activity benefits enormously from a hand on the shoulder or small group interaction; other parts, not so much. Some can be done just fine remotely; some cannot.

Today, teachers are pretty much expected to tackle all this as best they can, without much rhyme or reason. Whether delivering remote instruction, coping with a raft of student absences, or adopting new curricula, teachers are usually given a dollop of training and then told (to borrow the iconic Nike slogan), "Just do it!" This is partly about culture and management. But it's also hardwired into the current shape of the job.

In this chapter, we'll touch on a series of questions that can help us reconceive teachers' work. Why is it so hard to find enough qualified teachers? How else might we think about the shape of the teaching profession? Are there more promising ways to think about teacher preparation and pay? And how, if at all, can new digital tools help with all of this?

Exercise 3.1   Take a Step Back: Does Good Teaching Change When It's Virtual?

We frequently talk about "effective" and "ineffective" teachers. This tends to imply that these differences are stark and static. Yet the pandemic brought home just how slippery such assumptions can be. Some effective teachers had a terrible time pivoting to remote learning. Some things that make teachers successful in person just don't seem to translate online. Meanwhile, principals also observed that other teachers surprised them by flourishing online. What accounts for that? And what can we learn from it? This exercise works best in small groups and takes forty-five to fifty minutes. It can also work well as a kickoff for a more extended project.

How It Works

Small groups are asked to assume the role of a state advisory group convened to offer guidance on hiring, training, and supporting virtual teachers. The focus is on how virtual teaching differs from traditional classroom instruction and what to make of those differences. Small groups should take ten minutes to list five to ten practices, behaviors, characteristics, or skills that make a teacher effective in a brick-and-mortar classroom. The whole group should take a few minutes to discuss common themes. Then, give the small groups another ten minutes to make a similar list for a virtual classroom. Bring the groups together for a whole group discussion of the similarities and differences in the two lists. Which traits are equally relevant in the two environments and which are not? At this point, small groups should take another ten minutes to reconvene for a third time and talk about the virtual versus traditional contrast in terms of specific dimensions of teaching. How much do the differences depend on subject? On content? On teaching style? On age of the students? Ask groups to identify one key insight from each category. Gather the whole group and discuss where the small groups agree and disagree on the differences between classroom and virtual teaching. Finally, what do participants think might be done to better identify, train, and support teachers specifically for virtual environments?

Takeaways

Good teaching varies with context. Instructional strategies that work in intimate seminars may not translate to classrooms of thirty-five. Similarly, strategies that work when students are planted before a screen may differ from what works when teachers can put a hand on a shoulder, read a student's body language, or have a class up and about. The first takeaway is the need to consider when and how a teacher's personality, relationships, content mastery, tech savvy, or organizational acumen can be most effectively utilized. The second is that there is often real disagreement about which traits matter more for online or in-person instruction. And the third is that asking these questions—about what makes for good virtual teaching—is a powerful way to think more deeply about what makes for good teaching, period.

A PERPETUAL TEACHER SHORTAGE

Staffing schools today is no easy task. Public schools must hire 300,000 new teachers a year just to replace those lost to attrition. That's more than the total number of graduates produced by America's selective colleges each year. The constant need for new bodies makes it extraordinarily difficult for school systems to be choosy when hiring, strategic about assigning staff, or careful about training and preparation.

If you follow these things, you know that we've been in the throes of a perpetual teacher shortage for the better part of a half-century. The concerns took on heightened visibility in the wake of the pandemic and the ensuing "Great Resignation." By 2022, more than 90 percent of the nation's largest school districts said they were struggling with staffing shortages.[1] Things got so bad that, in 2022, the governor of New Mexico called out the National Guard to fill vacant school positions.[2]

Truth is, while the dislocations of the pandemic and its aftermath exacerbated staffing problems, much of the difficulty in recruiting teachers is a direct result of the profession's design. In the 1830s and 1840s, the leaders of the emerging Common School movement—most famously Massachusetts's Horace Mann—sought to expand basic instruction via schools staffed by plentiful (and poorly paid) female educators. Because Mann and his allies didn't quite trust their more feminized workforce, they initiated a system of bureaucratic licensure and administrative micromanagement to police these new hires.

The Common School crowd birthed a discount-rack approach to teaching that treated inexpensive female teachers as interchangeable, bequeathing us a cookie-cutter profession in which day 1 on the job looks pretty similar to day 5,000. Common School reformers also established a norm of capricious management. Back in the 1800s and early 1900s, teachers had no job security. Depending on the state and school system, they might be fired for being overweight, getting married, or having someone impugn their political beliefs. School leaders routinely based teacher pay on race, gender, and personal relationships.

Frustrated educators eventually revolted, winning (in the late 1800s) step-and-lane compensation, in which pay was based on credentials and experience, and (in the early 1900s) tenure protections. At the time, these reforms made good sense: step-and-lane pay and tenure were a big improvement over erratic, discriminatory leadership. Meanwhile, the combination of licensure, standardized pay, and sturdy job security proved to be a good match for the industrial best practices of the early- and mid-1900s.

The problem is that this blend of licensure, standardized pay, job protections, and (eventually) elaborate collective bargaining agreements has helped forge a rigid, batch-processed profession that is increasingly at odds with how professionals operate today.

Take the licensure system. Chad Aldeman of Georgetown University's Edunomics Lab has estimated that licensure requirements mean that training the average teacher costs about $25,000 and requires 1,500 hours. For possible career-switchers, working professionals who sacrifice current pay in order to pursue a credential, the cost is higher still.[3]

If it seems like this kind of system wasn't necessarily designed with the realities of contemporary school staffing in mind, well . . . you're right. For one thing, those nineteenth- and twentieth-century officials operated with a near-monopoly on educated women workers. Until about the 1960s, college-educated women had few professional employment options outside of teaching or nursing. Moreover, in an era when employees might spend their entire career in only one or two jobs, school leaders reasonably figured they didn't have to compete with other industries to incentivize teachers to stay.

Well, those assumptions started to unravel in the decades after World War II. As high school graduation became a universal norm, the teaching force increased apace—tripling from 1.1 million to 3.3 million between the 1950s and early 2000s. At the same time, amid this extraordinary hiring boom, K–12's monopoly on educated women came to an end. And, about that time, the idea that an employee might expect to start with a company in their twenties and do the same job for the next thirty years went from being a comforting convention to an odd anachronism.

Today, half of new teachers leave the profession in their first five years. While that sometimes gets treated as a crisis, it's actually pretty typical in a world where recent college grads routinely change jobs every couple years. Heck, at the associations, advocacy groups, and think tanks that hire recent college graduates to research and reform teaching, a five-year run is on the long side.

Unfortunately, policy makers and education leaders have been slow to respond to these shifts. It wasn't until the late 1980s that anyone really started to experiment with alternative licensure and midcareer recruitment. Meanwhile, efforts to reform pay have frequently had less to do with rethinking the profession than with tacking a test-score or master's degree bonus onto the salary schedule.

Rather than fervently wish that new teachers behaved more like they did in the 1950s, a Rethinker asks how we might reshape the profession to take advantage of a changing world. Today, schools still mostly rely on a staffing model that can no longer count on the reliable labor force of college-educated women that once made it hum. Whether that model was a "good" one is beside the point. What matters is that while it may have been well suited to the world of the 1950s, it's a poor fit for the world we inhabit today.

If we can't recruit our way to excellence, another popular hope is that we can train our way there. But the research on PD suggests that's an equally problematic bet. As a 2007 meta-analysis published by the federal Institute of Education Sciences (IES) reported, of 132 studies of PD, barely a handful offered "scientifically defensible evidence" of effectiveness.[4]

A massive 2014 IES follow-up found that just 2 out of 643 studies of math PD could show positive results that met conventional measures of research quality.[5] As the Brookings Institution's Tom Loveless has politely put it, "In a nutshell, the scientific basis for PD is extremely weak."[6] (I want to be clear: the point is not that professional development *can't* be useful; it's that we shouldn't expect PD to make a big difference given the shape of teaching as practiced today.)

Neither recruiting nor PD, as conventionally practiced, are promising strategies for turning Horace Mann's preindustrial staffing model into a good match for twenty-first-century schooling. Meanwhile, class size reduction efforts, the teacher evaluation craze of the Obama years, and a slew of efforts to add instructional coaches have consistently failed to deliver the hoped-for results. This is due largely, I suspect, to the fact that they've left intact the logic of "let's hire lots of teachers and ask them all to do a little bit of everything" and just tried to stitch the change on top.

WHAT SOCRATES CAN TEACH US

Teaching has not always been organized this way. Back when Socrates was doing his thing in ancient Greece, for instance, teaching was a simple proposition. Students sat and listened. Teachers talked and asked questions. That was it. It was pretty darn limited. It also meant that teachers had a chance to get very good at talking and asking questions.

From this dynamic was born the Socratic method, with its reliance on questioning, student response, and teacher feedback. It's the most basic approach imaginable for cultivating understanding and gauging what students know.

By asking questions, the teacher challenges students in ways that upend assumptions and illuminate ideas. The technique is often used to lead a student into contradictory statements, so as to surface complexities. Indeed, Socrates was skeptical about teaching via the written word precisely because he feared it would undermine this active student-teacher dynamic.

The Socratic method is intensely personalized. Done well, it involves constantly adjusting to the interests, limitations, and needs of each student at a given moment. In the hands of a skilled instructor, it's the most powerful model I've ever seen for promoting deep understanding and engagement.

So if we've got such an effective tool, why don't we see it used more often? And why does so much "Socratic" instruction wind up looking rote or ineffectual when we do see it?

It's not complicated: the Socratic method is really, *really* hard to do well. Lots of teachers may attempt it, only to engage in something that's more akin to a stilted question-and-answer session. The Socratic method requires that a teacher have deep knowledge of the specific topic, a library of relevant analogies, a mastery of the avenues the dialogue may take, and the ability to play devil's advocate (this last one can be extraordinarily challenging, even career-threatening, when it comes to sensitive, emotional topics).

Doing all of this well calls for time and practice, both of which are in short supply for teachers racing to cover the curriculum and juggle an armful of duties. It requires that teachers master a slew of analogies, rehearse various lines of argument, learn how to navigate fraught issues, and have the chance to observe what this looks like when it's all done skillfully. This is one of those instances when professional development—if properly designed, delivered, and targeted—could make a big difference. In practice, of course, few teachers get even a smidge of such training.

That's why few teachers are equipped to make good use of Socratic dialogue, even though it may be the very best way to explore some of the crucial topics that schools struggle to address today. Worse, trying to employ the Socratic method without training or practice can yield dismal results—and can prove toxic when it comes to sensitive subjects.

The Socratic method, *like every "learning technology,"* depends on the skill with which it's employed. This is the problem with asking every teacher to be a harried jack-of-all-trades. It means that even potentially powerful instructional practices are destined to disappoint, due not to their intrinsic flaws but to the burdens on the educators directed to apply them.

Exercise 3.2   Take a Step Back: Comparing Professional Models

This exercise is designed to help participants ponder the many ways in which professional work can be organized. A big challenge with rethinking teachers' work is that, even when teachers voice frustrations about their job, they're frequently not sure how else things might be arranged. Truth is, there are many ways for professions to order tasks, shape professional cultures, and structure careers, and some alternatives may hold a lot of promise—for both students and educators. This exercise works best in small groups and takes about twenty-five to thirty minutes.

How It Works

Break participants into small groups and give them fifteen minutes to compare the composition of staff at a given school to that in a law firm, architectural firm, or medical practice. What do they notice about the job descriptions? The number of people who hold different jobs? (Note: This is the rare instance where it's fine for participants to pull out their phones and Google freely, since the point is partly to learn a bit about how these different organizations are staffed.) Point out that law firms or hospitals have staffing gradations among practitioners that look very different from those found in schools. At law firms, junior associates have a very different job than do senior partners, while the practicing lawyers are outnumbered by paralegals and legal secretaries. In a hospital, a small number of specialized physicians work closely with huge numbers of nurse practitioners, registered nurses, emergency medical techs, and so forth. After participants have had the chance to look a little more closely at these other approaches, give the small groups five to ten minutes to discuss the pros and cons of these models. How might each model affect the quality of work and the lives of the practitioners? What are the trade-offs? Could elements of these models work well in schools? Finally, gather the whole group for five to ten minutes to share their reflections and reactions.

Takeaways

Knowledge-based professions organize work in different ways, and there should be nothing untoward or unusual about exploring and then weighing the merits of other models. In many ways, *teaching* is more reflective of the assumptions of a factory-model, cookie-cutter approach than these other skilled professions. Participants should come away appreciating that there's not one right staffing model for a given profession but that there are a variety of approaches that may suit.

CONTEMPLATING THE MEDICAL MODEL

Education isn't the only profession that needs to make the fullest use of talented, trained professionals. It can be instructive to ponder how the others do it. I find it especially helpful to think about how this works in medicine.

About 8 million people work in US schools; nearly half of them are teachers.[7] On the other hand, while there are about 9 million medical professionals in the United States, not even a tenth of them are trained doctors.[8] Those specialized physicians are, however, surrounded by a wealth of complementarily trained colleagues.

Medicine didn't always look this way. A little over a century ago, there was no such thing as a medical specialty, and it was hard to talk seriously about medical expertise. Today, physicians receive intensive, tailored training in nearly two hundred specialties. (By the way, this can offer some insight into why teacher PD so often disappoints. If physicians were just trained broadly to be doctors, it'd be tough for training to be specific enough to be all that useful.)

The kind of exquisite training that doctors receive is possible, in large part, because only a sliver of medical professionals are trained for those roles. The lion's share of those who work in medicine are not doctors but physician assistants, nurse practitioners, registered nurses, emergency medical technicians, and the like. These professionals are appropriately trained, but less intensively and expensively than doctors.

These differently skilled individuals are organized to work as a team. Support staff aren't asked to tackle tasks that exceed their expertise. Meanwhile, exquisitely trained physicians aren't spending time on routine tasks that can readily be handled by colleagues. Cardiovascular surgeons don't spend time taking blood-pressure readings, filling out patient charts, or negotiating with insurance companies; these responsibilities are left to nurses or staff. And no one expects physician assistants or emergency medical technicians to occasionally step into the operating room and perform cardiovascular surgery.

While it'd be nuts to suggest that medicine has the right staffing model, there is much here that could help school leaders rethink how to make the best use of professional talent. The point isn't to import medicine's precise hierarchies, work routines, or paper-chasing pathologies but to ask what we might learn from medicine about leveraging talent, experience, and training.

In schooling, things work very differently than they do in medicine. More times than not, for instance, elementary principals will tell me that literacy is their top priority—that it's crucial that kids are reading comfortably by the end of second grade. Yet, ask an elementary principal to give you a look at their best second-grade reading teacher and you'll almost invariably see that teacher teaches reading for ninety minutes—and then teaches art for thirty minutes, polices the cafeteria for twenty-five, takes their turn at bus duty, and all the rest.

I've found that principals rarely see anything odd about any of this—at least until asked what they'd think of a hospital that had its cardiovascular surgeon doing cardiovascular surgery just ninety minutes a day and spending the rest of the day doing patient intake, delivering meals, and organizing medical supplies.

Bottom line: if employees have scarce skills, it's worth taking full advantage of them.

By doing nothing more than rethinking the use of staff time, schools could conceivably get thirty-five hours a week of great reading instruction from that one terrific reading teacher—*five times* as much as before—while ensuring that many more students get access to high-quality literacy instruction. And it's a fair bet that, if roles, pay, and responsibilities were reordered sensibly, the teacher would be happier, more professionally fulfilled, and feel like they were making fuller use of their talents.

Now, some readers may well be thinking, "Whoa! Hold up. Remember 'Chesterton's Fence' from chapter 1 and that whole warning about avoiding reckless change? I think it's important that elementary kids be with one teacher for most of the day—I worry about undermining student-teacher relationships." It's a terrific point. There are schools where K–5 specialization works wonderfully, but there's also evidence from Indiana, for instance, that elementary specialization can have negative consequences.[9]

In the end, the right question isn't whether something like specialization "works." It almost undoubtedly will in some schools and not in others. The better question is whether there are more promising ways to employ skilled staff in a given school. So Rethinkers proceed deliberately, asking whether a given change might do more harm than good, but not allowing such concerns to become an excuse to avoid the essential questions.

Exercise 3.3   Check Your Understanding: What Teachers Do (and Don't) Want

This is one of the simpler exercises in the volume. It's a chance to make the conversation about what teachers do less personal, by focusing on what teachers nationally say they'd like to do more or less of. This also serves as a pretty good setup for exercise 3.4. It works best in small groups and takes about ten to fifteen minutes.

How It Works

Put participants into small groups and give them five minutes to discuss and answer two simple questions: What are the top three things teachers say they want more time for? And what are the top three things teachers say they want to spend less time on? After participants discuss in their groups, have each group share its guesses before the facilitator reports the results. Then, take a few minutes to discuss. (Note that the data come from a national survey conducted in 2022. This means the results will invariably change over time and also that they won't necessarily reflect the situation in a given school or system. The answers aren't *right*, but they do offer a useful window into what teachers say.)

The Answers

In 2022, when the Merrimack College Teacher Survey asked a national sample of teachers what they wanted to spend more time on, the top responses were more planning time (29 percent), actual teaching time (28 percent), and time for collaborating with colleagues (17 percent). Nothing else cracked double digits. When asked what they wanted to spend less time on, teachers said general administrative tasks (31 percent), nonteaching student interaction (22 percent), and PD (12 percent). Again, nothing else cracked double digits.[10]

Takeaways

Regardless of the precise answers (which will vary from place to place and over time), these sorts of questions are helpful for thinking about how teacher time is organized. How much time do teachers say they have for preparation—and how much time *should* they have? How much time are teachers spending on administrative tasks, assessment, or discipline, and how much should they be—and should that vary by teacher or role? The answers offer a practical tool for exploring how professionals experience their day-to-day routine. If such information isn't collected locally, it should be, and this survey can provide a potential model.

START WITH WHAT TEACHERS DO

Teachers perform many, many different tasks each day. They lecture, facilitate discussions, grade quizzes, monitor hallways, fill out forms, counsel kids, struggle with obstinate technology, and much else. When I ask teachers to list what they do in a typical week, groups can list dozens of tasks in short order. Heck, special education teachers regularly spend 40 percent of their time filling out paperwork (and, in some cases, additional hours each week driving from school to school). And elementary teachers can report that as much as a quarter of classroom computer time is lost to technical difficulties and forgotten passwords.

In 2022, teachers reported working an average of fifty-four hours a week—with just under half spent directly teaching students.[11] If teachers are already shouldering a full load, doing more of one thing necessarily means doing less of another.

In chapter 2, we discussed the OECD data on school time. Well, it's not only America's kids who spend a lot of time in school; the same is true of teachers. In 2021, at every level of K–12 schooling, American teachers taught at least two hundred hours a year more than the OECD norm. By international standards, teachers in the United States spend a *lot* of time in classrooms.[12]

And yet, I'm struck how little attention gets paid to how this time is used. What's happening during that extra two hundred hours? How diligently are school leaders protecting teacher time from distractions? These questions should be routine. Yet, my experience is that they don't get much sustained attention.

When I work with teachers, they almost invariably report that they've never been part of a disciplined effort to unpack what they do each day. In my experience, school and system leaders rarely make it a point to examine how teachers are actually spending their time. That makes it tough to know if time is being used effectively, to identify where technology can be a time-saver, or to assess the division of labor.

In Japan, for instance, in order to minimize transition time, many schools have all students eat lunch in their classrooms, and the teachers move room to room during the day while students stay seated. Japanese teachers also have much larger classes than their American peers but that, in turn, means they teach fewer hours and have much more planning time. Is such a model better than ours? Worse? How does one weigh the trade-offs? These are questions that should occasion far more reflection than they do.

Exercise 3.4   Take a Step Back: What Teachers Do All Day

When we're used to doing something, it can become so routine that we cease to notice it. This exercise can be good at sparking discussion about priorities and the use of time. This exercise complements the time diary exercise from the last chapter (exercise 2.3) but is more interactive and moves the focus from documentation to asking whether teachers are spending their time on the things that are most valuable. It works best in small groups and takes about twenty to twenty-five minutes.

How It Works

Give each group a piece of poster board and a marker. Groups should identify all the discrete tasks they can think of that they (if they're teachers) or that their staff (if they're school or system leaders) performed in the past week. The point is to unpack particulars, meaning that "teaching" or "grading" aren't sufficiently precise responses (for instance, groups should specify all the different kinds of teaching that took place, whether that's large group, one-on-one, remote, or what have you). After ten to fifteen minutes, have the groups pause and circle the five tasks that take up the most time. This gives them a chance to consider which activities are one-offs and which are actually time-consuming. After about three minutes, instruct groups to star the five activities that they deem most valuable for students. Finally, give the whole group a chance to discuss. (A perfectly satisfactory prompt is usually a simple: "What did you notice?")

Takeaways

The sheer amount of stuff teachers do in a week is vaguely intuited but rarely made clear. This exercise can drive discussion of which tasks are more or less useful. Three key insights tend to emerge. First, when the stars and circles don't line up (and they usually don't), it's a stark illustration that many teachers aren't spending their time on the things they think matter most for kids. Second, teachers really juggle an astonishing number of tasks, and that can make it tough to focus. Third, getting a window into all this can be eye-opening for school leaders and administrators, who are frequently shocked to hear that teachers are spending so much time on a given task.

ALTERNATIVE VISIONS OF THE TEACHING JOB

As noted at the start of this chapter, one big problem with teacher retention is the lack of professional opportunity. For too many teachers, day 5,000 looks like a facsimile of day 5. Heck, for many teachers, the primary route to professional (and financial) advancement is to go into administration—a nutty system that either takes veteran educators *out* of the classroom or else leaves them feeling unappreciated and undervalued.

Keeping this challenge in mind can be useful when it comes to rethinking the teaching job. There are a bunch of promising ways to go about it, all of which entail taking a fresh look at roles, responsibilities, work routines, and compensation.

North Carolina–based Public Impact's "Opportunity Culture," for instance, allows teachers with a track record of exceptional student achievement to take on the role of "Multi-Classroom Leader." They continue to teach classes (although with a reduced load) while leading and mentoring small teams of teachers. Rather than play the relatively hands-off role of grade-level leader or department chair, lead teachers are responsible for the student outcomes of teachers on their team and are compensated accordingly. They're empowered to select and evaluate their team members and oversee a cluster of classrooms where they provide mentoring, monitoring, and support.[13]

Another model is the "New Teacher Workforce" initiative developed at Arizona State University's Mary Lou Fulton Teachers College. This approach features teams of educators abandoning the one-teacher, one-classroom role to take advantage of their complementary strengths. Instead of four third-grade teachers each being responsible for one-fourth of a hundred third graders, the school assesses those one hundred students' learning needs and assembles a team of educators to meet them. Teams include education leaders, professional educators, para-educators (teaching assistants with specific skills), and community educators (volunteers of various kinds).[14]

Many schools have also explored a blended school model that embraces remote teaching as a regular, structured part of the curriculum. As we've noted, the pandemic illustrated that many teachers may be more successful in person than virtually but that, for others, the reverse can be true. Moreover, there are persistent shortages of teachers in some subjects—particularly higher-level math, science, and world languages. Incorporating regular remote instruction allows schools to take full advantage of educators who don't live locally, don't want to commute, or aren't able (or willing) to work a traditional school schedule. We'll discuss such models more fully in the next chapter.

Another option is to create "operations associates" who work alongside teachers. The idea is to rebalance the duties of teachers and support staff in the same way that medical practices apportion the duties of physicians and nurses. Much like the New Teacher Workforce's "community educators," these staff support school-day transitions and duties, tasks that can amount to full-time work for non-college-educated adults. Jobs include morning drop-off, bus duty, hallway transitions, meals, recess, monitoring for truants, and disciplinary support. Staff are trained in school culture and have the chance to build meaningful relationships with students, while freeing teachers to devote more time to instruction.

There are plenty more such ideas worth exploring. Of course, these are possibilities, not recipes. School leaders shouldn't feel obliged to explore any one approach, but they *should* regard these models as a challenge to ask how schools can make better use of skilled staff.

WHAT ABOUT TEACHER PAY?

Some readers are thinking, right about now, "Well, this is all vaguely interesting, but what about teacher pay? The real problem is that teachers aren't paid enough."

That's partly right.

Inflation-adjusted teacher pay did indeed *fall* by an estimated 3.8 percent over the last decade.[15] That's a huge problem. Good teachers are woefully underpaid, have few attractive professional pathways, and rarely enjoy the respect or professional opportunities they deserve. It's easy to appreciate what prompted the wave of teacher strikes that commenced when West Virginia's teachers walked out in early 2018, seeking a modest 5 percent pay bump in a state where median pay was under $45,000 a year.

There's widespread agreement that teachers should be paid more and that terrific teachers should be paid much more. That said, it's *not at all* clear that cheapskate taxpayers or inadequate funding are the problem.

After all, even as after-inflation teacher pay fell during the two decades between 1992 and 2014, *after-inflation* school spending rose by 27 percent (during a period that included the 2001 dot-com crash *and* the 2008–2009 Great Recession).[16] So, where'd the money go? Most of it went to adding staff, employee health care, and retirement benefits. Those dollars *were* spent on employees, just not on boosting take-home teacher pay.

For example, in West Virginia, even as student enrollment fell between 1992 and 2014, nonteaching staff increased by 10 percent. Nationally, while student enrollment grew 19 percent during those years, nonteaching staff grew more than twice as fast.[17] Heck, across the nation, from 1950 to 2009, while student enrollment doubled, the ranks of nonteaching staff grew *sevenfold.*[18] New dollars that could have gone to boosting teacher pay instead went to adding staff.

Here's one way to think about it. In 1970, we had an average student-teacher ratio of about 27 to 1. Today, the ratio is about half that, or about 13 or 14 to 1. Based on long experience, I suspect some readers are saying, "That's nuts! Our class sizes are nowhere close to that." If that's your reaction, take a moment, go to your district website, check the number of students, and divide that by the number of teachers. Having been through this exchange many, many times, I'm confident the student-teacher ratio will be less than 15 to 1.

Now, note that we're talking *student-teacher* ratio and not class size; even as schools have added staff much more rapidly than they've added students, it hasn't dramatically reduced actual class size (due to contract provisions and staffing practices).

Relative to the number of students in school, we've roughly *doubled* the number of teachers since 1970. Alternatively, we might've kept student-teacher ratios level and instead put those new dollars into doubling teacher pay.

If we'd done that, *average* teacher pay in the United States in 2021 would've been over $130,000. In fact, it'd have been more like $150,000, since schools would only have to make health-care and pension contributions for half as many teachers. Now, while some may find these numbers hard to believe, understand that *this is not a controversial calculation!* (It's based on the annual salary figures compiled by the nation's largest teacher union, the National Education Association.)[19]

Revisiting the quantity-quality trade-off raises all kinds of intriguing questions. If we relied on fewer highly paid teachers rather than more lower-paid ones, it would make selective recruiting and careful training more possible. A Rethinker suspects that this could be good both for students and for the profession's stature.

A LESS CLOISTERED SCHOOLHOUSE

A single-minded focus on recruiting new college graduates for teaching jobs once made sense, back when college-educated women were a captive applicant pool and it was routine for new college grads to settle into a job for a long haul. Today, though, it's increasingly bizarre for schools to fixate on training and recruiting twenty-two-year-olds in the hope that they'll stay in the job into the 2050s. Even worse, the costly and complicated licensure apparatus still doesn't offer any assurance that teachers are ready for the job.

The nation's 1,200-plus teacher-preparation programs (traditional and alternative alike) are time-consuming but of suspect quality. They do little to screen applicants for academic performance.[20] Researchers have found no demonstrable difference in performance between certified and noncertified teachers.[21] And supervisors also don't seem to think licenses mean much. The Aspen Institute has found that just 7 percent of superintendents and 13 percent of principals think certification ensures that a teacher "has what it takes" to be effective in the classroom.[22]

Licensure systems (in tandem with seniority-based pay) also make teaching inhospitable to career-changers. While midcareer professionals move freely between most jobs, entering teaching requires enduring the licensure gauntlet and then starting at the bottom of an inflexible pay scale. This doesn't make much sense, given the skills, maturity, and savvy that a veteran engineer, journalist, or staff sergeant might bring to the classroom. Indeed, professionals who enter teaching in their thirties or forties (or fifties) may well be more confident in their career choice and, in today's workforce, could easily wind up teaching for decades.

Thus it's no surprise that the pandemic led many states to explore loosening the licensure chokehold.[23] There are many ways to make it easier for career-changers to demonstrate competence or for states to streamline the path to professional entry. Tennessee, for instance, has launched an apprenticeship program allowing school systems to recruit and train teachers outside of the usual licensure apparatus. This allows candidates entering the teaching field to stay in the workforce, collecting a paycheck and sidestepping student loans. Making the profession more welcoming to those who can't afford to take time out of the workforce also turns out to be a recipe for broadening and diversifying the potential teaching pool.[24]

Schools made their peace with a host of nontraditional educators during the pandemic when they relied so massively on parents and guardians. And, in the aftermath of COVID-19, tutors played an outsized role for systems seeking to provide students with essential support. A less bureaucratic licensure regime could give school leaders more freedom to hire the staff they need while giving veteran educators more room to provide hands-on (and appropriately compensated) mentorship. For Rethinkers, such a shift isn't a last resort; it's a chance to think more creatively about how schools might benefit from a vast wave of untapped talent.

RETHINKING TEACHING

There are lots of promising ways to strengthen the profession, if we free ourselves of Horace Mann's clammy grip. That includes thinking differently about how teacher jobs are defined, the role that veteran educators play, and how complementary staff are used.

Of course, it's not like rethinking the teaching profession is a new idea. Al Shanker, Ted Sizer, Deborah Meier, Adam Urbanski, and many others were offering visions of a reshaped profession in the 1980s, 1990s, and early 2000s. Many promising ideas (from career ladders to peer review) have gotten lots of tryouts, only to yield meager results. A Rethinker suspects that's because these efforts flew in the face of existing policies, practices, and contracts. New duties were piled atop old. Nominal titles came with little real authority and little additional compensation.

A few years ago, for instance, would-be reformers spent a lot of energy trying to more precisely rate teachers via complex formulas designed to reflect how a given teacher's students fared on state reading and math tests—in the hope that they could then use those results to drive decisions about tenure and teacher pay. It was an approach seemingly calculated to promote rigidity and micro-management. It all felt more like how encyclopedia salesmen were paid in 1965 than how professionals are typically evaluated or compensated in the twenty-first century.

Even weirder was that the whole evaluation mania involved very little attention to how effective teachers might be put in a position to have a bigger impact on students. Setting aside all the problems with using math and reading scores as the be-all and end-all for gauging teacher performance (even for teachers who taught world languages, history, or a nontested grade), the whole crusade seemed blindly trapped in Horace Mann's schoolhouse.

A very different model is on display, for instance, in South Korea's tutoring culture, where the most in-demand tutors can make millions of dollars a year teaching at the country's private *hagwons* (cram schools). Their financial success is partly a product of the massive stakes attached to South Korea's highly competitive national test, but also because talented tutors have the flexibility and freedom to serve huge numbers of students—by employing assistants, leveraging digital tools, and providing each student with a more limited slice of time.

Tutoring is not *the* answer. It is, however, another way for an array of educators to leverage their strengths, on their schedule. It's one more way to attract talented professionals to this work and to cultivate a rich system of mentoring and support.

I recall once talking to Richard Rusczyk, founder of the Art of Problem Solving, about his online tutoring service for high-level math. He told me that his stable of tutors included some big-dollar Wall Street traders who otherwise would never interact with high schoolers. But they enjoyed the chance to teach advanced math part-time and many of them were quite good at it. The more of this there is, the better for students and educators alike.[25]

The Rethinker seeks a profession that attracts a wealth of talented teachers, supports them in myriad ways, and makes the best use of their talents to instruct and mentor students by redesigning the roles they play. Whether or not this fits our conventional mental picture of "teaching" just doesn't matter much. And it certainly shouldn't hold us back.

CHAPTER 4

Technology Rebooted

When it comes to education technology, we ping from tech mania to frustrated disappointment and back again. My inbox is filled with a steady stream of excited missives hyping some new learning technology. Yet, as historian Larry Cuban has wryly observed, education technology tends to be "oversold and underused."[1] Indeed, in just a moment, I'll go so far as to suggest that there's been only one education technology that's ever really delivered.

Meanwhile, the pandemic's duct-taped, wholesale remote learning didn't do education technology any favors. Harried school leaders responded to school closures by throwing classrooms online—telling unprepared teachers to essentially move their classroom onto a screen filled with glazed-eyed, muted kids.

Some schools even implemented a widely reviled practice (derisively termed "Zoom in a room") in which masked students sat six feet apart in classrooms staring at screens, supervised by a nonteacher, while their teacher taught remotely. The approach managed to be simultaneously mindless and dehumanizing—a perfect encapsulation of technology gone wrong.

Given all this, does it even make sense to suggest that digital tools can help schools after millions of students, parents, and educators saw first-hand the problems with shoddy remote learning? The answer: it depends. Personalized digital tutoring that uses engaging exercises to build phonemic awareness is a very different creature from a remote classroom in which an instructor is trying to foster a lively discussion with twenty-four muted students.

Put another way, remote learning during the pandemic was about replacing things. It wasn't redesigning or improving the learning experience. So, most of the time, a class discussion was replaced by an awkward Zoom session. A book was replaced by a PDF. Classroom work was thrown online as an asynchronous assignment. This was the same stuff, just with the humanity vacuumed out. That's always going to make for a worse experience. It also completely misses the promise of technology.

What does that promise look like? Well, when I taught high school, back in the *last* century, there were pretty much two kinds of tutoring options: you could talk to a student through the phone mounted on your kitchen wall or you could drive to meet the student somewhere. The phone calls were rarely helpful and the logistics of face-to-face meetups were hugely limiting. Today, in everything from chemistry to Korean, students can readily access virtual face-to-face tutoring from skilled experts around the globe, for something like $20 or $25 an hour. *That* kind of virtual learning used to be impossible. Technology has made it possible. Designed skillfully, it can have a *profound* impact.

Of course, that requires education technology to actually work, smoothly and consistently. Consequently, it's a wonder technology providers don't devote way more resources to supporting the day-to-day use of their products. As one veteran educator sighed, "At our school, they always have technical experts on hand if something breaks, but they rarely have tech instructional coaches who can help us use the tech to its highest potential. It's strange."

When it comes to schooling, the right measure is not just how well technology is designed but how well it's used. And Rethinkers have a host of questions on that score.

Exercise 4.1   Take a Step Back: Then Versus Now

One recurring challenge with education technology is the need to focus on what's useful rather than what's cool. That can make it worth pausing to consider how technology is used in a field outside education. My go-to exercise for this (because it's both amusing and evocative) is seeing how pit stops in professional racing have evolved over time. This exercise works best with small groups and takes twenty to twenty-five minutes.

How It Works

Find a video of the Indianapolis 500 from 1950 and a video from a contemporary race. (I like to use the YouTube video "Formula 1 Pit Stops 1950 & Today," found at www.youtube.com/watch?v=RRy_73ivcms, but it's fine to use an alternative.)[2] Show the clips back to back. The initial reaction is usually surprised laughter, as participants see that a pit stop process which took more than a minute in 1950 takes only a few seconds today. The question: What made that possible? Groups should take five minutes to list changes they observed with regard to tools, technology, roles, and coordination. Then run the videos a second time, with participants keeping an eye out for what they might have missed the first time. (Typically, they'll note a bunch of additional things on the second go-round.) Try to spot the concrete changes that technology has made possible, especially how it's altered tasks and teamwork. Take a few final minutes for a whole group discussion about what it would mean in practical terms to translate these kinds of changes to a K–12 environment.

Takeaways

New tools and larger crews have allowed pit stops to become exponentially faster. But schools have also added new technologies and staff, without seeing similar benefits. What should we make of that? Is it a reflection of *how* we've used tools and staff? Participants should be sure to note the specific differences on display: How tires are changed. Where members of the pit crew stand. That the pit crew did away with the frenzied windshield wiping. The fact that cars are no longer permitted to refuel during the race. This is about participants training themselves to notice specific, incremental changes (that can collectively deliver big benefits), all of which offers a stark contrast to education's familiar, grandiose talk of "transformational" change.

ED TECH'S BLEAK TRACK RECORD

The siren call of "innovation" can obscure the reality that *how* technology gets used often matters more than the invention in question. That's why so many gadgets are endlessly hyped and just as endlessly disappointing. For a century, reformers have promised that each new technological advance will transform schooling. Take the case of film. Schools first used films in 1910; by 1931, twenty-five states had departments dedicated to educational film and related media. In 1922, Thomas Edison predicted, "The motion picture is destined to revolutionize our education system. In a few years it will supplant largely, if not entirely, the use of textbooks." Things didn't quite work out that way.[3]

Then there was radio. In 1923, New York City's Haaren High School was the first to use the radio for classroom instruction, broadcasting a lecture to an accounting class. By 1931, there was a radio division in the US Office of Education.[4] By 1932, nine states were regularly airing educational programs. Benjamin Darrow, an official with a New York education innovation fund, wrote the 1932 book, *Radio: The Assistant Teacher*, billing radio as the "vibrant and challenging textbook of the air." By the 1940s, more than half of all schools had radio equipment, and the director of the Cleveland public schools' radio station promised that "a portable radio receiver will be as common in the classroom as is the blackboard." Yet, for all that, principals said that radios weren't all that useful due to scheduling difficulties and the fact that programming wasn't linked to the curriculum.[5]

Next came television. In the 1960s, President John F. Kennedy got Congress to provide $32 million to develop classroom television. By 1971, over $100 million in public and private funds had been spent on educational television (despite surveys that showed teachers weren't using the televisions in class). Students spent more time visiting the bathroom than they did actually watching televised lessons. When teachers did use TV, there was a dearth of meaningful preparation, deliberate follow-up, or lesson integration.[6]

In the twenty-first century, the song has stayed the same. In 2000, at the height of the millennial tech boom, Maine governor Angus King made a splash by giving laptops to all of the state's seventh graders. The goal, he explained, was to "do something different from what everybody else is doing."[7] Perhaps not so surprisingly, there was zero evidence that the $50 million program had an impact. Studies of laptop giveaways in other locales have found similarly disappointing results: as part of the international One Laptop Per Child Initiative, the nation of Peru spent $200 million distributing laptops to 800,000 students, only for a 2012 study to find no evidence that the effort improved learning—and some evidence it may have *widened* achievement gaps.[8]

Years ago, a leading technology consultant confided to me that his greatest frustration was that school system leaders devoted more energy to acquiring gadgets than to how they use them. As he put it, "We see districts buy 1,000 iPads and deploy them out to the schools. They get all excited and the parents get excited. But the schools don't know what to do with them."

What's the lesson from all this history? Every time a Rethinker hears someone lauding the potential of a new technology, they should pose three questions. What will it take for this technology to deliver for students? What has to change for that to happen? What could go wrong? The promise of any new education technology rests on those answers.

Exercise 4.2   Check Your Understanding: Oversold and Underused?

For those intrigued by education technology, there's a tendency to enthuse about things like "flipped classrooms" and "blended learning." But there's a long history of new tools failing to live up to bold claims. Our tendency to forget this gloomy history fuels overpromising and leads us to underestimate what it'll take for new tools to deliver. This exercise can help on that count. It works best in small groups and takes twenty to twenty-five minutes.

How It Works

The small groups should list as many education technologies as they can in five to ten minutes. (Most of the time, groups initially name things like Chromebooks, laptops, iPhones, and desktop computers, and then, with a little prodding, move on to VCRs, TVs, radios, and such.) Encourage groups to keep adding to the list, leading them to incorporate things like chalkboards, pencils, and the book. Then ask groups to take ten minutes and go through their list, giving each technology an A to F letter grade for how revolutionary its potential was and another grade for how revolutionary it proved to be in practice. Finally, ask each group to identify the technology for which there was the biggest gap between potential and impact, discuss why that was, and think about what would've changed it. (Another good question is how each new technology would've been graded when first introduced versus how it's regarded today.)

Takeaways

At least three realizations tend to emerge. For starters, over time, the most successful technologies (like books or chalkboards) get so enmeshed in classroom practice that we cease to even think of them as a "technology." Second, ease-of-use matters greatly. It doesn't take much training or coordination to use the chalkboard; on the other hand, aligning radio lessons with classroom curricula and schedules proved so tricky as to be impractical. Third, headaches related to workability mean that *potential* benefit tends to have only a limited relationship to *practical* benefit. A new tool may work great in a boutique environment on a trial basis, but that doesn't necessarily tell us much about its likely real-world benefits.

JOBS TO BE DONE

Given the history, many educators view classroom technology with well-deserved suspicion. Rather than making their work more manageable, new tools frequently create hassles (think glitchy software, lost laptops, forgotten passwords, Wi-Fi outages, and kaput AV systems). This means digital tools are frequently more distracting than helpful. Just count the number of times a given student discreetly eyeballs videos or browses shopping websites during class.

All this was taken to some ridiculous extremes during the pandemic. Teachers grew exhausted trying to devise engaging lessons for a parade of virtual classrooms dotted with camera-off, muted, pajama-clad students. By a two to one margin, teachers said they were more "fatigued" than "invigorated" by technology during the course of COVID-19.[9]

At the same time, there are obviously plenty of things that educators need and want technology to do. For instance, RAND researchers have found that 80 to 90 percent of teachers say they routinely use homemade materials or those they've found online (most often via Google or Pinterest).[10] Teachers wind up cribbing together instructional resources, even as school systems spend heavily on curricular materials that sit on the shelf.[11]

The problem is that because school leaders and tech vendors aren't really sure what kind of tools would help, teachers wind up using the stuff that does exist in this sort of makeshift fashion. A terrific explanation of this phenomena was offered by former Harvard Business School professor Clay Christensen via his notion of "Jobs to Be Done." Christensen explained that, for new technologies to really deliver, there needs to be a clear sense of the job they're being "hired" to do.[12]

Thomas Arnett, a former math teacher who studies technology in schools, has written extensively about how Christensen's approach applies to schooling. Arnett observes that teachers want convenient, easy-to-use tools that can replace "cobbled-together workarounds," but that's not what they get. Instead, they are encouraged to abandon time-tested strategies for the unproven and time-consuming. Arnett observes, "If a 20-minute tutorial gave [teachers] what they needed to incorporate an attractive new resource or practice into the next day's lesson, they would give it a shot. But if adoption required 12 hours of training and a complete overhaul of their unit plans, they weren't interested."[13]

Veteran teachers spend years developing strategies and resources, while newer teachers scrambling to keep up rarely have much appetite for mastering unwieldy new technologies. It's a no-brainer, really. When asked to dump things they know in favor of the complicated and untried, it makes sense for teachers to react with skepticism. If teachers are to view technology differently, it needs to be offered up with an eye to the jobs they need done.

WHAT THE BOOK CAN TEACH US

The key issue is less with the technology than with how it's been dropped into schools. After all, a tablet can offer access to dynamic, world-class instruction or it can be an excuse for students to covertly watch cat videos. The difference depends on how the technology changes what students and teachers actually do all day.

Consider history's most potent bit of education technology: the humble book. I mentioned earlier that there's only one piece of ed tech that's ever delivered on the big talk of "transformation." This is it.

The introduction of the book, made possible by the invention of the printing press in the mid-1400s, provided readers previously unthinkable access to experts from around the world. It enabled students to learn things *even if their teachers didn't know them.*

The book also made it possible to reimagine the schoolhouse. With books, students could master content and concepts outside of school, learning even when a teacher wasn't there to instruct them. Books allowed students to reread passages when necessary, to move at their own pace, and to learn in the evening, when ill, or when assigned to a teacher who was unskilled or uninteresting. While a book may well be inferior to a riveting demonstration delivered by a gifted instructor, for most students books were a vast improvement over having to attend a teacher's peroration.

In "flipping" the classroom (by allowing students to absorb material at home), the book empowered teachers to work in new ways. They could lecture less and explain, mentor, or facilitate more. Rather than spend a whole class reciting content, teachers could ask students to read at home and devote class time to the kinds of dynamic inquiry that engage young minds and help students make sense of the content. The book was not simply an occasion to do more of the same, only slightly better; it enabled a fundamental reimagining of how teachers teach and how learners learn.

Of course, the fact that teachers *could* do these things was no assurance that they *would*. Even today, five centuries on, it's not uncommon to see teachers providing tedious, low-quality lectures in which they spend class time repeating to students the very things contained in their textbooks. Whether that's because the students aren't reading the book or because the teacher hasn't figured out how to build on what the students have read, it's an important caution: there are no guarantees that even terrific tools will be used effectively.

Moreover, despite its many benefits, the book has real limitations. For one, the content and language of a given text will inevitably be too difficult for some readers and too easy for others. For another, while students learn best when eye and ear work in tandem, books are a silent medium. And, of course, books have fixed content, which prevents them from offering a live demonstration or alternative explanation to a confused reader.

New digital tools can help with all this. Online materials can be updated rapidly, customized to a student's interests and reading level, and incorporate exercises that let students apply new concepts and receive immediate feedback. Digital resources can embed short explanatory videos, supplementary materials that address frequent points of confusion, and picture-heavy explanations for students who are struggling with a word or concept.

Today's digital tools can take the book's strengths and amplify or augment them. That's what the book did to the oral narratives and papyrus rolls that came before. While there may be little in education that is wholly new, the right tools can enable exploration, engagement, instruction, and the accumulation of knowledge in ways that were previously impossible.

Exercise 4.3   Take a Step Back: Was the Book a Big Deal?

The previous exercise (exercise 4.2) dealt with technology that gets oversold. This exercise addresses a technology that is too easily taken for granted. Today, education technology is frequently discussed in terms of labels (e.g., Chromebooks, iPhones, 3D printers) rather than functions. That's a problem. Rather than focus on what a tablet does and doesn't do, we wind up talking about whether a school has *enough* tablets. A good way to address this tendency is by contemplating a simple, familiar technology: the book. This exercise works best with small groups and takes about twenty minutes.

How It Works

Break into small groups and start with each group discussing the prompt, "Was the book a revolutionary learning technology?" Give groups five to ten minutes to brainstorm and list the reasons it *was*. The goal is to get participants thinking about what it means for a technology to be revolutionary. Then, have them pause and give them another five minutes to list the reasons that the book *wasn't* revolutionary. Finally, take another five to ten minutes for a whole group conversation in which participants share their reflections.

Takeaways

Typically, the "yes, it was revolutionary" stance wins out (much to the surprise of participants who sometimes chuckle at the initial question). That's a useful prompt for reflecting on what makes technology transformative. Participants should emerge understanding that the book first made it possible to flip the classroom by allowing students to read at home and then engage in more active learning at school (even if, five centuries on, many classrooms don't make great use of that capability). At the same time, participants should ponder what it takes for any technology to actually deliver on its potential. This exercise can nudge participants away from thinking in terms of "before ed tech" and "after ed tech" and toward appreciating the need to think about technological tools in terms of what they actually do.

TECHNOLOGY'S REAL PROMISE

Good schools are intimate, trust-based, intensely personal institutions, and education technology must be designed with that in mind. Interactive smartboards that seamlessly allow teachers to call up digital lessons while engaging with students are terrific. But when teachers are distracted by the challenges of getting images to display while muttering that glitches make them miss the old marker-and-eraser whiteboards, something has gone awry.

Useful digital tools start not with technical specifications, cool features, or nifty new applications, but with a clear-eyed appreciation of technology's strengths. The fancy term for this kind of thinking is "user designed"—it starts with intense research into what users need. (Unfortunately, while this approach is routine in the development of consumer technology, it's much less common in education technology.)[14]

When it comes to how technology can be useful, there are at least three big opportunities it presents.

New Opportunities to Personalize Learning

The notion of "differentiated instruction" has immense appeal. It should. It seeks to give students instruction that's geared to where they actually are and what they need. But it's also really hard to do. When I taught high school, I had something like 150 students a day. Even if I'd been far more seasoned, organized, and adept than I was, I'd have found the practical challenges of differentiation overwhelming. The problem wasn't a lack of desire; it's that juggling everything necessary to differentiate instruction for that many students is just really difficult.

Technology can make it more feasible for teachers to personalize assignments, offer level-adjusted instruction, and assess learning. At the same time, by making this work more manageable, it can give teachers more time to focus on the uniquely human elements of teaching (whether that's discussing an essay, listening to a student's frustrations, leading a Socratic discussion, or providing tailored instruction to a small group).

Today's digital technologies are capable of providing a dazzling array of explanations, illustrations, cartoons, games, tutorials, exercises, and assessments, all informed by learning science. This marks a profound change from a world where the textbook discussion is necessarily fixed and immutable, even though different learners might benefit from alternative explanations or demonstrations. These tools make possible more personal learning, in which teachers spend more time mentoring students and less time batch-processing them.

New Opportunities to Meet Student Needs

While there's much talk about the value of tutoring today, "tutoring" can entail a lot of different things (just as we noted in chapter 3 when it comes to teaching). It may mean students need a single answer checked at 11 p.m. or a complicated formula explained. Many times, what a student actually needs is a real-time three-minute explanation more than a tutor. Today, that kind of support is available in a way it wasn't before.

Consider Brainly, an online platform launched in 2009, which helps answer homework questions in subjects including math, history, English, biology, chemistry, physics, social studies, geography, health, arts, and business. With more than 350 million student users around the globe, it enables students to help one another, search for existing answers to millions of common questions, or ask experts for rapid responses. User ratings, a network of moderators, and volunteer monitors help police the process.[15]

Platforms like Brainly are also exploring how to harness artificial intelligence, such as with features that allow students to snap a photo of a math problem and immediately get a step-by-step explanation. Such tools raise inevitable, important questions about whether they're being used as shortcuts rather than learning aids. Such tensions deserve careful consideration. At the same time, a Rethinker is cognizant of the potential value of providing students (especially those who don't get it at home) with bite-sized, user-friendly, instantaneous support.

New Opportunities to Make Learning Accessible

As former senator and Harvard University scholar Daniel Patrick Moynihan famously observed, producing a Mozart quartet two centuries ago required four musicians, four-stringed instruments, and, say, thirty-five minutes. And that's still true. Moynihan's point was that some things aren't improved by technology.

But Moynihan's analogy was incomplete. He was right about that quartet, but what his line elides is that the number of people who can *hear and appreciate* a given performance has increased exponentially. Today, the public now has access to performances once available only to a privileged elite. While listening to a digital recording of world-class musicians isn't the same thing as watching them perform live, it's a lot more accessible and affordable (and, potentially, more appealing to those who'd rather listen in comfortable surroundings or at their leisure).

Schools can struggle to find high-quality teachers in math, science, special education, and world languages. But new technologies make it possible to extend the reach of terrific teachers, leverage far-off professionals, and offer high-quality curated resources—even in hard-to-staff fields. Pixels can't replace a hand on a shoulder or a dynamic classroom discussion. But technology can provide access to well-designed tutorials, cogent instructors, and engaging mentors that students would otherwise never encounter.

ENVISIONING A NEW KIND OF CLASSROOM

What does it look like to use technology to rethink the practice of teaching and learning? New Classrooms, a middle grades math model employed by more than a hundred schools, offers one instructive illustration. Launched over a decade ago as a pilot program in New York City, New Classrooms leverages digital tools and a team-based teaching model to allow students to learn and progress at the pace that suits them.

New Classrooms works from the premise that marching a class of students through the scope and sequence of a grade-level math curriculum each year has a slew of downsides. Many students don't get enough time to master essential skills or content, while other students sit through whole days spent covering things they already know. Student absences can create big problems, while teacher absences tend to bring learning to a halt.

By unpacking a state's grade-level math learning objectives, separating out the component parts, and then building a technological backbone to help students proceed more expeditiously, New Classrooms offers a vision of how this can work differently. Before school starts, students are assessed to gauge what they do and don't know. New Classrooms then employs an algorithm that uses the pretest and other data to identify which objectives students already know, which they need to master, which ones they should tackle next—and draws on an expansive menu of options to suggest an instructional approach for a given objective based on each student's needs and history.

As noted in chapter 1, it can be useful to understand all this in terms of the difference between digital music and an old LP record. Fifty years ago, to hear a song, you'd have to go out, buy the full album, and play it through. Digital music changed all that. Today, we call up one favorite song after another or just let algorithm-driven playlists track our preferences.

That same customized intuition shapes the New Classrooms model, which uses those pretests; brief, near-daily unit assessments; and varied instructional tools to meet the needs of a hundred-plus learners. Depending on the unit and the day, a given student may be engaged in large group instruction, small group instruction, one-on-one tutoring, independent study, or computer-assisted instruction. The organizing algorithm juggles all this so as to make the fullest use of teacher and student time.

Students can skip over objectives they've already mastered and then tackle more advanced content using the instructional approaches that work best for them. This allows students to spend as much time as they need to master learning objectives, when necessary, and to race ahead, when appropriate. This is a case of technology making practical the vision of student-centered instruction touted by educators like Ted Sizer and Deborah Meier many decades ago.[16]

The possibilities are obvious. For starters, teachers are typically absent eight or nine days a year. Learning no longer needs to grind to a halt on those days (this alone adds more than a week of learning time each year). When students are absent or struggle to master a concept, teachers are no longer required to scramble to catch them up; there's the time and flexibility to meet learners where they are.

Teachers have more latitude to play to their strengths, while shared interactions create more opportunities for team members to observe and mentor one another. And incorporating online tutoring, intensive computer-assisted exercises, and the like also enables teachers to devote more time to small group instruction, personal coaching, and other innately personal roles. All in all, it's an approach rife with the promise of rethinking.

Exercise 4.4   Imagine If: Making Competency-Based Learning a Reality

In chapter 2, we discussed the appeal of measuring learning based on mastery rather than time. We also noted, though, the challenge of making competency-based learning practical in schooling, especially for subjects where the scope and sequence is less clear-cut. Finding ways to tackle that reality is essential if competency-based learning is going to play a significant role in K–12. This exercise encourages participants to do just that. It works best in pairs and takes thirty-five to forty-five minutes.

How It Works

Pairs should start by taking a few minutes to talk about their general feelings regarding time-based versus competency-based learning (if anyone in the group is unfamiliar with the notion of competency-based learning, it's a good chance to review the concept). Give pairs five minutes to settle on one subject they'd like to see shift from a time-based to a competency-based model in their school or system. They should be specific. What grade level? If it's high school math, science, or history class, which course do they have in mind? Once groups have done that, they should take ten minutes to explain *how* they'll decide what content is essential. (Note: pairs are *not* trying to map out the essential content, though that can make for an eye-opening larger project.)

Again, each pair is simply trying to determine *how* they'll figure out what's essential. Will they survey practitioners or college professors? Ask disciplinary bodies? Empower local teachers to decide? Have the whole group discuss the ideas for five to ten minutes. Then give each pair another ten minutes to discuss how they'll determine what constitutes mastery. Will it be a standardized test? A portfolio? Something else? If it's a test, what percentage of the information will students need to know? If it's a portfolio, what will have to be included and how will work be judged? Finally, reconvene the whole group to spend about ten minutes discussing the assessment question.

Takeaways

When asked how they feel about competency-based versus time-based learning at the outset, most participants are usually enthusiastic about competency-based. By the end of the exercise, they're much more skeptical. One insight here is the staggering gap between liking an idea in theory and being comfortable with how it'll work in practice. This exercise also tends to yield three specific intuitions. First, this kind of drill can sharpen our understanding of what subjects entail and point to principled disagreements about what is and isn't essential. Second, it illustrates why it can be so difficult to move from a time-based to a competency-based model and underscores the significance of getting the particulars right when it comes to measuring learning. Third, while the challenges posed by figuring out competency are vital for any attempt to rethink time, they're essential if approaches like badges or digital delivery are going to become part of the fabric of K–12 schooling.

THE VIRTUAL LIFE

Virtual reality is a very cool thing, with its goggles, gloves, and 3D vibe. The question for educators is whether it's good for teaching and learning. On that count, there's obvious potential. The immersive learning company Strivr, for instance, is focused on making virtually accessible those activities—including learning experiences—that would otherwise be "rare, impossible, dangerous, or expensive."[17]

The Stanford University School of Medicine has used immersive virtual reality for surgical training. It allows students to explore the brain and practice complex surgeries without ever touching an actual patient or cadaver. The programming can generate interactive three-dimensional images that allow surgeons to map the contours of a patient's brain (using MRIs, CT scans, and angiograms) before surgery ever begins. When virtual reality lets *brain surgeons* do that, imagine the kinds of rich, accessible, 24/7 career and technical opportunities it can offer when it comes to fields like welding, automotive repair, nursing, or carpentry.[18]

Illustrating what's possible, Dreamscape Immersive has launched a virtual reality learning program with Arizona State University and Steven Spielberg. In "Immersive Biology in the Alien Zoo," freshman biology students examine an alien animal called a "frogcat" that lives in a virtual jungle. The frogcat's offspring are sick, and in order to cure them, students explore, test hypotheses, interact with peers, and collect and analyze data. Tackling hands-on science in an alien world introduces competitive stakes into science class, highlights the utility of biology and chemistry, and infuses science with an applied, vocational component. The early results suggest the course is delivering on at least some of that, boosting engagement and outcome mastery.[19]

Virtual reality may allow students to engage in complex, otherwise-dangerous chemistry experiments, study ancient Rome by walking its streets and talking to passersby, traverse the ocean depths, or stroll the halls of the Louvre.

Of course, virtual reality deserves the same scrutiny as any technology. The logistics, including acquiring and maintaining the headgear, can be a hassle. Will that change as the technology gets streamlined and more sophisticated? How about if students are using virtual reality during nonschool hours? Would such developments make the use of educational virtual reality seamless or simply further aggravate concerns about digital overload? Whatever the technology, Rethinkers are always more interested in such questions than in naysaying, excited huzzahs, or self-serving vendor assurances.

IT'S NOT VALUES VERSUS TECHNOLOGY

While the back-and-forth between techno-enthusiasts and techno-skeptics can give the impression that educators must choose a side, a Rethinker asks if schools can take advantage of new tools *and* cultivate timeless, human values. This shouldn't be that hard to figure out. After all, from papyrus scrolls to pencils, educators have *always* employed the technologies of the moment.

A provocative, appealing notion of tech has been sketched by Marina Umaschi Bers, a professor of computer science and human development at Tufts University. In her 2022 book *Beyond Coding*, Umaschi Bers urges approaching education technology and computing with an eye to human connection and values. She explains, "I teach robotics to a five-year-old so that she can grow into a *mensch*, a Yiddish word describing a person of integrity and honor."[20]

Her point is that how we use technology reflects and shapes our values. Individuals can use the same kinds of digital tools to support a vulnerable family via GoFundMe or to defraud them in a phishing scam. The values reside not in the technology but with the users.

Umaschi Bers recommends thinking about technology in terms of a creative "playground" rather than a more stilted "playpen." As she puts it, playgrounds are environments where we create, express ourselves, and "learn new skills and problem-solve while having fun." Playpens? They're hemmed-in, anodyne places where toddlers peer at the world around them. When you watch a rambunctious robotics competition, you're seeing kids on a playground. That's worlds apart from battling buggy software to access online materials. If technology seems to be sucking the humanity out of a school, it's a pretty good sign that the tech is being misused.

During the pandemic, the Silicon Schools Fund, a California funder, dug into what its schools were doing and realized that what mattered most was whether remote learning was, well, human.[21] Silicon Schools CEO Brian Greenberg makes the simple point: "Where teachers lecture to empty Zoom boxes, it's virtually impossible to make remote teaching effective." He recalls watching classrooms where, after thirty minutes, students hadn't been asked to contribute to the chat box. When students are virtual, it's that much more important that they're seen and heard.[22]

The choice cannot be *between* digital tools and humane schooling. Imagine telling any educator in an earlier era that their classroom could be value-driven *or* make use of newfangled technologies like chalkboards and books. Any thoughtful educator would say, "That's a dumb way to think about things." That was true a century ago, and it's equally true today.

DON'T POOH-POOH THE PERILS

While it's goofy to suggest that new technology is, by default, a bad thing for schools or students, there are legitimate concerns about its impact. While today's wired world may offer extraordinary benefits, it's also ushered in an array of problems, including cyberbullying, new forms of peer pressure, and social isolation.

As psychologists Jean Twenge and Jonathan Haidt have observed:

The smartphone brought about a planetary rewiring of human interaction. As smartphones became common, they transformed peer relationships, family relationships and the texture of daily life for everyone—even those who don't own a phone or don't have an Instagram account . . . It's harder to strike up a casual conversation in the cafeteria or after class when everyone is staring down at a phone. It's harder to have a deep conversation when each party is interrupted randomly by buzzing, vibrating notifications.[23]

The rise of the smartphone and social media coincided with abrupt shifts in youth emotional well-being. The share of teens who report getting together nearly daily with friends dropped by nearly half between 2000 and 2015, with time spent instead on social media and gaming.[24] Whistleblowers at social media giants like Facebook (now Meta) and Instagram have revealed that they've long known their products were wreaking havoc on teens' mental health and self-image.[25] In 2021, a multinational study of more than a million adolescents found that, between 2012 and 2018, loneliness increased in thirty-six out of thirty-seven nations. Loneliness wasn't linked to unemployment, gross domestic product, income inequality, or family size, but rose in tandem with smartphone access and internet use.[26]

Meanwhile, kids have been spending more and more time online. In 2015, high school seniors spent six hours a day online (aside from time spent online for school); that included two hours a day texting and an hour and a half gaming. That 2015 figure was twice what it had been in 2006.[27] In 2019, Common Sense Media found that eight- to twelve-year-olds spent nearly five hours a day watching TV, playing music, gaming, or on social media; for thirteen- to eighteen-year-olds, the figure was more than seven hours a day.[28] In 2021, researchers reported that, during the pandemic, *aside* from school-related screen time, twelve- to fourteen-year-olds said they spent 7.7 hours on a screen each day—including 2.6 hours gaming and 2.4 hours streaming.[29]

What does all of this mean for schools? One response is to say, "Well, it's an online world. Kids are online all the time anyway, and this is mostly a matter for families—schools can't single-handedly address tech overload." Another is to say, "Kids are getting too much device time, they're visiting unsavory places, and they're engaging in toxic activity. It's bad for their development and threatening their mental health. Schools have to play a role."

Suspecting both sides have valid points to make, the Rethinker tends to respond with questions. Can schools more effectively promote student well-being by reducing screen time or by teaching students to navigate it? Do students fare better when schools use less technology? Does digital activity shorten attention spans, and how might schools combat that? Is one-on-one virtual mentoring qualitatively different from the same experience in person?

A Rethinker is open to the possibility that the answers may ultimately vary, across students or settings.

RETHINKING EDUCATION TECHNOLOGY

Things that look cool but don't actually add value are the stuff of late-night infomercials. Too often, that's the technology of the schoolhouse as well.

For technology to make a difference for students and teachers, it needs to be a tool for rethinking what students and teachers do and not just a stop-gap slapped atop familiar routines. There's a terrific illustration here from *banking* (of all places!).

When banks first introduced ATMs, the new machines didn't actually improve service, cut costs, or make it easier for customers to access their money. Why? It's because they were glitchy, complicated, and most importantly, located *inside* banks. You still had to visit one of the bank's branches during regular banking hours. It was only when banks realized ATMs could be made simpler, sturdier, and located *outside* that they could be used to extend hours, add more locations, and allow banks to operate with fewer tellers. It wasn't the technology—it was how it was used.[30]

The ATM story makes me think of all those schools that used to have a storeroom where a dozen or more dusty TVs sat on mounted carts, only to be rolled out occasionally when a substitute teacher was showing a movie. Or schools where students use laptops to create dazzling PowerPoints but know more about the templates and animation than the science on their slides. Education technology is too often more about the technology than the education.

But it needn't be that way. Seeking a purposeful, disciplined use of technology at school? Just visit that mecca of pedagogy: the office of a power-house high school football coach. Not too long ago, coaches taught players the plays they'd run by drawing lots of Xs and Os on a chalkboard. They showed them the opponent's plays in grainy footage on the locker room VCR. They coached blocking techniques by yelling really loud.

Now? Find a successful team and it's a good bet that players are studying preloaded plays on tablets, meaning coaches no longer need to diagram each play by hand. Players are spared the time they used to spend sitting while coaches erased one play and chalked up the next. And they can more readily visualize how plays are supposed to unfold via animated Xs and Os (which can be played at normal speed, in slow motion, or paused at any point). Rather than the whole offense or defense watching those grainy VCR cassettes en masse, players watch videos tailored for their position. A coach can now pull out an iPhone, film a player attempting a new technique, and immediately review the result with that player. Technology is improving the player-coach interaction and letting players learn in more personalized ways.

It's not the technology that matters—it's what we do with it. If used to connect students with mentors; engage families; provide access to richer, more rigorous instruction; and make better use of student and teacher time, then technology can be a powerful tool. Conversely, employed in tedious and alienating ways, even the niftiest technology can become a mortal threat to good teaching and learning.

There's a choice here. And it's one that Rethinkers are eager to seize.

CHAPTER 5

Choice Reconsidered

We've discussed how rethinking the role of staff, technology, or tutoring can allow for more engaging, personalized learning. Of course, all this is easier said than done, especially when it requires every school and system to figure it out for each student. Embracing a more expansive set of educational options (or choices) can help by offering more opportunities to meet the needs of students and more freedom for educators and communities to rethink schooling.

Now, much of the time, talk of school choice tends to unfold as a weird morality play in which one is either for empowering parents *or* for supporting public education. The resulting debate manages to miss much of what matters. It ignores that all kinds of choices are hardwired into American public education. It skips past the fact that the affluent already choose schools when purchasing homes, meaning the debate is really about the options available to everyone else.

And the fevered arguments are disconnected from what most families care about. In the course of the pandemic, for instance, when schools closed and millions of families were told they needed to keep their kids home, there was little interest in abstract debates about school choice or homeschooling. Indeed, conventional demarcations—between "home" and "school," "public" and "private," and "teachers" and "parents"—were scrambled.

During long stretches of off-and-on remote learning, mandatory masking, and makeshift summer offerings, families were focused on whether their options met their needs. Some parents, frustrated that their district school seemed nonresponsive or slow to reopen, sought out charter schools or private school options. Others, concerned about health risks or protecting vulnerable family members, wanted assurance they'd have continued access to a remote option.

Little of this was about "school choice." It was about solving problems.

The fact that families want more options doesn't mean they dislike their local schools (much less, that they're eager to flee them). In 2022, for instance, more than three-quarters of parents said that they were satisfied with their child's experience in a public district school *even as* more than seven in ten endorsed education savings accounts, school vouchers, and charter schools.[1] In short, parents overwhelmingly like both their child's public school *and* school choice policies. They don't see a tension.[2]

How can that be? How do we reconcile parent support for more choices with affection for their local public schools? It's not hard, really. Parents like having options. They may seek alternatives when it comes to scheduling, school safety, or instructional approach. They want to be able to protect their kids from bullies or school practices they find troubling. At the same time, though, parents may also value schools as community anchors, like their kid's teachers, and live where they do precisely because they like the local schools.

Families can embrace options without wanting to abandon their local public schools. The notion that one is either for empowering parents *or* for supporting public education is a misleading one. Real parents don't think this way.

So, how does a Rethinker approach the school choice debate? The same way as anything else: by not getting sucked into sweeping ideological claims but by asking how expanding options might help meet the needs of students, families, and educators.

CHOICE IS WOVEN INTO THE FABRIC OF AMERICAN SCHOOLING

Amid today's partisan sniping, it can be easy to forget that educational choice has been woven into the fabric of American education from the nation's earliest days—long, long before charter school policies and school voucher programs were adopted in the early 1990s. There've been plenty of efforts to constrain parental choice, of course, and the resulting tensions have also long been part of our educational tradition.

During the colonial era, it was presumed that most children would get only a rudimentary education, and that only a tiny handful of affluent white families would choose to have their sons pursue more formal education (frequently to prepare for the ministry). Schools were routinely located in churches, and local church leaders were charged with choosing the school-teacher. In that era, the notion that there was any tension between parental choice, the role of religion, and public provision would've been deemed an odd one!

In the 1800s, in response to the unapologetic anti-Catholicism of the Common School movement, an expansive parochial school system took root in the United States. It soon spawned fierce debates as to whether education funds should support the education of students who chose to attend parochial schools. While local churches had long played a leading role in public schooling, the rise of parochial education made such blurred lines newly controversial. By the 1880s, in an appeal to anti-Catholic sentiment, presidential candidate James G. Blaine championed a constitutional amendment that would bar public funds from supporting religious schools.

While Blaine's amendment was unsuccessful (as was his presidential bid), many states would go on to adopt their own "Blaine amendments." In the early twentieth century, Oregon took the crusade against Catholic education one step further. Urged on by an ungainly alliance of progressive education reformers and the Ku Klux Klan, Oregon outlawed private schools, only for the Supreme Court to rule (in *Pierce v. Society of Sisters*) that it couldn't do so. In recent decades, in cases like *Zelman v. Simmons-Harris*, *Trinity Lutheran v. Comer*, and *Carson v. Makin*, the Supreme Court has ruled that the First Amendment's free exercise clause means states can't exclude religious schools from state programs for which they're otherwise eligible.

In the early twentieth century, progressive reformers, troubled by what they viewed as the unseemly influence of immigrants and the poor, sought to buffer public schools from parental influence. They consolidated schools into larger districts, made school board elections nonpartisan, and moved those elections to dates designed to minimize turnout while insulating school system bureaucracies.

The reins of these systems were handed to a professional caste of administrators trained in the new art of "scientific," factory-style management. This push to emulate the then-innovative management of Ford Motor's centralized assembly line had some success limiting parental input. Ultimately, though, in the years after World War II, parents of means found alternative ways to make choices on behalf of their kids.

As suburbia grew and yellow school buses became a fixture on the nation's landscape, families responded to opaque school bureaucracies by buying homes with more of an eye to choosing a school. This aggravated dispari-ties as the middle class and the affluent gradually opted into suburbs while the less affluent were left behind.

By the 1970s and 1980s, in response to white flight and the travails of forced busing, magnet schools and public school choice plans had become popular tools to combat segregation. Both Republican and Democratic officials saw these programs as a way to redress unconscionable education inequities. Those same years saw major victories for the hugely successful fight to legalize homeschooling.

In addition to choices *between* schools, the post–World War II era also gave rise to choice *within* schools. During the postwar years, educators had to serve a growing school population with an immense variety of needs. That fueled the expansion of vocational education, the post-1970s explo-sion of special education, and a growing array of high school electives. By the 1980s, University of Michigan scholar David Cohen and his colleagues were writing about the challenges of the choice-infused "shopping mall high school."[3]

In recent decades, as charter schools have grown to enroll more than 3 million students, the tapestry of options has expanded to increasingly include scholarship (or voucher) programs, education savings accounts, microschools, course choice options, hybrid homeschooling, and more. A Rethinker is less interested in polemics about all of this than in asking how these options can better serve the needs of students, families, and educators.

THINKING MORE EXPANSIVELY ABOUT CHOICE

Choice isn't only an integral part of the American education landscape—it's embedded in public schools themselves. From start to finish, schooling is a stew of choices made by parents, students, educators, system officials, and policy makers. Parents choose whether to send their children to preK, when to start kindergarten, or whether to opt their child out of sex education. Stu-dents choose groups and activities, which electives to take, and many of the books that they'll read. Teachers choose where to work, which materials they use, and how to deliver instruction. District staff choose policies governing discipline, curricula, field trips, and attendance zones.

Outside school, we take for granted that families will choose childcare providers, pediatricians, dentists, babysitters, and summer programs. Indeed, many such choices involve parents or guardians making decisions that are subsidized by government funds. And the choices they make will have big implications for their child's health, well-being, upbringing, and education. All of this tends to be regarded as wholly unexceptional.

Exercise 5.1   Check Your Understanding: What Parents Want

What do parents actually want in a school? I've long been struck by how often I'm in conversations about school improvement that unfold without anyone ever directly addressing this question. This exercise focuses participants on the question of what parents say matters most when choosing a school. It works best in small groups and takes about twenty to twenty-five minutes.

How It Works

Organize participants into small groups and give each group five to seven minutes to list the ten factors that they think parents are most concerned about when choosing a school. Next, give them three minutes to rank those factors from most to least important. After developing that list, present the survey results shown in figure 5.1 and ask each group to take a few minutes to compare those numbers to their predictions. (Note: the results are informative but *should not be treated as "right."* After all, local views may diverge from the national average, poll results are always imprecise, and results can change over time.) Finally, take ten minutes to talk with the whole group about what the answers were, what they noticed, and what surprised them about the different responses offered by public and private school parents.

The Research

These results (see the figure) are from EdChoice's invaluable national surveys (they're so valuable because parents are too rarely asked about all this).[4] When asked what they look for in a school, the figure shows what parents in public and private schools had to say (they could give more than one answer).

FIGURE 5.1   Top factors for choosing a school among public and private school parents

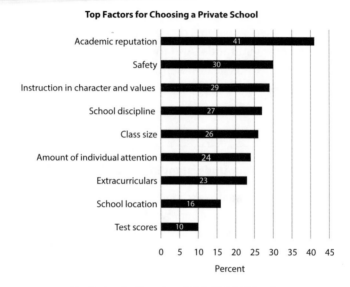

Top Factors for Choosing a Private School

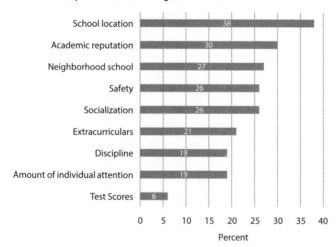

Top Factors for Choosing a Public District School

Source: Drew Catt, John Kristof, and Colyn Ritter, 2022 *Schooling in America* (Indianapolis: EdChoice, 2022), 21, https://www.edchoice.org/wp-content/uploads/2022/11/2022-SIA-powerpoint-FOR-WEB-3-FIXED.pdf.

Takeaways

After accounting for factors like location and peers (public school parents especially emphasize proximity), parents pay particular attention to academic reputation and school safety. Meanwhile, parents say they don't attach nearly as much importance to test scores, class size, and diversity. What to make of this? For starters, the things that educators and advocates are *used* to talking about may not be the things that parents say they care most about. While parents are not always "right," it matters if schools are focused on things that aren't important to families. If educators think that test scores, class size, or diversity matter more than parents seem to, that should be acknowledged and discussed. Either way, it's vital that educators spend time thinking these issues through. (If they haven't, it's an excellent reason for a school or system to start regularly surveying local parents.)

Now, there used to be a lot more limitations on the choices that students, families, and educators could make. For the whole of the nineteenth century, and most of the twentieth, it was a struggle just figuring out how to get students, books, and teachers together under one roof. At a time when transportation and communication were limited, it was hugely inconvenient for students to enroll at a school outside the neighborhood and impractical for educators to offer an array of specialized school or course offerings.

Today, those constraints are dusty memories. New tools have made it possible to communicate, share materials, deliver instruction, manage data, assess learning, and coordinate in ways that were once unimaginable. Textbooks are no longer a bottleneck. Virtual tutoring no longer seems like science fiction. And after millions of students were remote for more than a year, taking select classes from far-off online instructors no longer seems especially novel. This has all eroded notions of where the schoolhouse ends and choice begins.

These changes hold great promise for educators who may be frustrated with the inertia of impersonal, stifling routines. After all, if one spends much time talking school improvement with educators, you'll regularly hear phrases like "I'd like to do this but the contract requires this" or "I'd love to do that but it's not allowed." The same options that appeal to families can empower teachers and school leaders who feel stuck in unresponsive schools or systems. Educators, like parents, can value public education while wanting more opportunities to find or create learning environments where they'll be free from entrenched rules, regulations, contract provisions, and customs.

THE LESSONS OF LEARNING PODS

Learning pods offer one intriguing way to rethink the boundary between schooling, tutoring, and afterschool support. A learning pod is a handful of students who study together, under the auspices of a tutor, outside of a traditional school setting (mostly to augment school-based instruction rather than replace it). Learning pods leaped into the public eye during the pandemic as families caught up in remote learning sought to provide their kids an organized, intimate, and supportive environment.

Now, learning pods might be an artifact of COVID-19 and easy to see as a bit of a "that-was-then" time capsule. Fair enough. Even if that ultimately proves to be the case, though, there are some terrific takeaways here for a Rethinker.

The tens of thousands of learning pods that emerged across the country were most commonly described as something akin to sustained, high-intensity tutoring. Kids got customized attention in a comfortable, face-to-face environment. While learning pods may have been largely makeshift, more than half of families and three-quarters of instructors said they preferred their pod experiences to prior experiences in school.[5]

Researchers studying learning pods found that, by three to one, parents said that their kids felt more "known, heard, and valued" than they had in school and that, by two to one, children were more engaged in their learning. Contrasting the intimate pod experience with the "anonymity" of school, one parent explained, "There's no getting lost in this. In the pod, there's no sneaking by without getting your work done like there would be in school."[6]

Pods also tapped new pools of instructional talent. More than half of instructors had not been working as certified classroom teachers when the pandemic started: they'd been tutors, nannies, paraprofessionals, or retired educators. But it turned out that parents thought highly of these instructors, with four in five saying their child was at least as likely to receive high-quality instruction in their pod as in school.[7]

The teachers liked pods, too. Consider the experience of Samantha, a former classroom teacher and principal who launched a learning pod for five students in grades 1 through 4 who repeatedly toggled between remote and hybrid instruction. She described the experience not as exhausting but as energizing: "This is probably the most professionally satisfied I've ever been in my entire career," she said. "[After] this experience, I'm not going back to formal K–12 education. I can't."[8]

Samantha's experience was hardly unique. Instructors who'd previously taught in traditional school environments said they were more satisfied with their work in a learning pod (by a margin of better than four to one) and felt like they had more supportive relationships with families when it came to student learning (by better than ten to one). Teachers talked about curricular flexibility, financial benefits, and an enhanced sense of autonomy.[9] One-third of pod instructors said they had no interest in pursuing a traditional teaching role due to concerns about rigidity and red tape.[10]

But learning pods also had all manner of limitations. They typically cost around $300 a week and were only available to those families with the acumen and resources to create them. Instructors had no administrative support, tech assistance, disciplinary backup, or organizational infrastructure. Parents frustrated by a teacher's behavior or instructional practices had no recourse other than quitting the pod and scrambling to find an alternative. Pod arrangements could be fragile, with blowups among participants potentially leaving students without a teacher or teachers without a job.[11]

So, are pods a good idea? It depends. It depends on what they're used for and how they're constructed. But it's not hard to imagine them providing more intensive support or an alternative learning environment for students who are struggling in a conventional classroom. School systems could help interested parents find one another, connect with local resources, and locate a qualified instructor; such aid could be especially valuable for low-income or non-English-speaking families, who might find the option appealing but struggle to organize or finance learning pods on their own.

Exercise 5.2   Imagine If: How to Make Choice Work for Everyone

When it comes to educational choice, one challenge is that families may have trouble taking advantage of the various options. Parents who don't speak English, aren't literate, or don't know how to find information about schools may not be in a position to make informed choices. The goal of this exercise is to spark fresh thinking about how schools and communities can address those challenges. This is typically done with small groups in about forty to fifty minutes, but it's also the kind of exercise that can work especially well as a group project over the course of a week or two.

How It Works

Small groups assume the role of a school district task force charged with ensuring that all local families have the resources to make informed choices. The aim is to provide families with useful, up-to-date information on their education options, *including both* those options that involve changing the school a student attends *and* those that don't (as with charter teachers or course choice). Give each group fifteen minutes to sketch the kinds of programming or support that might be helpful. Groups should start by cataloging the variety of in-school and between-school options that exist locally, considering the kinds of information they want to provide, and discussing how that information will be made available. Groups should consider what's distinct about choosing among options that are all housed in a single school as opposed to choosing between different schools, and what resources can help parents with different types of decisions. Then give each group another ten to fifteen minutes to sketch out the particulars of what their plan would entail. Finally, ask each group to do a brief three-minute presentation of their strategy and close by discussing the similarities and differences of the various proposals.

Takeaways

The nice thing about this exercise is that it shifts the conversation away from a debate about whether participants are for or against school choice and toward the practical question of how to help all families take advantage of the options that already exist. It's a reminder that the promise of educational choice very much depends, for good or ill, on information and the support that parents can draw upon.

MICROSCHOOLS AND CHARTER TEACHERS

Microschools are *really* small schools that provide the opportunity to radically rethink the teacher's role and the contours of the schoolhouse. Microschools typically have a few dozen students (or even fewer), with students typically attending in person. The schools employ one (or a handful) of teachers to lead instruction. Unlike most learning pods, microschools aren't supplemental programs; they *are* a child's school.

For students lost amid the oft-impersonal rhythms of institutional life, the intimate scale can be reassuring. This kind of environment may be a more natural fit for students who struggle to behave or stay engaged in a conventional classroom. It can allow for more personalization, parent-teacher collaboration, or advanced learning than the standard schoolhouse allows.

At the same time, microschools pose a host of challenges. How do they handle infrastructure? Teacher absences? Coverage of a full curriculum? What would it look like for school or system leaders to organize internal microschools and how would that work? The answers are very much a work in progress.[12]

In chapter 3, we noted some of the ways in which teaching might evolve to empower educators and create more room for professional growth. Well, one particular version of microschooling that fits this bill is the "charter teacher" model. Teachers would be able to obtain state-granted authorization to operate autonomous classrooms *within* traditional district schools. Charter teachers would have wide latitude to hire assistants, choose how many students to instruct, decide how many classes they'd teach, and determine their own instructional model. Teachers would agree to be held accountable for student outcomes, and they would only teach students whose parents choose to enroll their child with that teacher.[13]

For a sense of how this might work, consider the pediatric model. Pediatricians typically work in partnerships, have a significant say when it comes to scheduling and hiring support staff, and choose how many patients to serve. At the same time, of course, patients are free to choose their pediatric practice and their pediatrician. (In one sense, the charter teacher approach simply democratizes access to the choose-your-teacher machinations regularly employed by connected parents who know how to pressure principals and work the system.) Teachers disenchanted with large bureaucracies would have more control over their work while more flexible or part-time options might just draw former educators back into the profession.

The charter teacher model isn't currently in use. Putting it into practice would require state officials to establish a process by which teachers could demonstrate professional mastery or a record of high student achievement. Qualified teachers could obtain small grants to launch their own practices, after which they'd be funded on a per-pupil basis developed by the school district.

How would all this work in practice? Well, a teacher might contract with a district to accept up to thirty-eight sixth graders, while receiving 50 percent of the per-pupil outlay for each (the other 50 percent would go to the district for administration, transport, materials, facilities, and such). In Arlington, Virginia, where I live, that teacher would receive about $350,000. She might choose to work with two teaching assistants and to pay them $45,000 each, plus benefits, and then retain about $240,000 to pay her own salary and benefits—for a salary of close to $200,000.

Should a given district embrace microschools or pursue a charter teacher model? It depends. As I've said, the goal here isn't to champion any particular program or policy. But these models offer intriguing opportunities to meet student needs and empower talented educators. And that's catnip to a Rethinker.

HYBRID HOMESCHOOLING

It may be hard to fathom today but a half-century ago, homeschooling was *illegal* across most of the United States. A series of legal and political battles in the 1970s and 1980s changed that. By 2020, more than 3 million children a year were being homeschooled, a number that increased dramatically during the COVID-19 pandemic.[14] But just what does it mean to homeschool a child?

While the term "homeschooling" may bring to mind a picture of a parent and a child sitting at a kitchen table, most homeschool families make extensive use of networks, online resources, and tutors. Indeed, the difference between homeschooling and a learning pod (or a microschool) is often just a matter of degree.

In the wake of the pandemic, there was broad interest in education options that incorporate more of what homeschooling provides. In 2022, two-thirds of parents with children in special education said they'd like a school schedule that had their child learning at home at least one day a week (though just 15 percent of parents wanted to do *full-time* homeschooling). Among other parents, more than half said they'd like to have their child home at least one day a week.[15] Oh, and just over half of teens said *they'd* like to learn at home at least one day a week.[16]

In other words, lots of parents and students are interested in maintaining some of the parent-child interaction they experienced during the pandemic but don't want to be "homeschoolers." Hybrid homeschooling seeks to provide what those families seek, with students enrolling in school for part of the week and learning from home for the other part. More than a thousand hybrid homeschools have emerged across the country in recent years. Many are private schools, others are charter schools, and a handful are part of traditional school districts.

The arrangements can play out in many ways. A hybrid homeschool might have students in the building four days a week, with different classes (or grades) of students learning from home on different days. It might have all students learning at home on Mondays or Wednesdays or on certain mornings or afternoons. Some schools are more prescriptive when it comes to curricula while others leave more to parent discretion. For younger children, parents generally play a much larger instructional role while there's more independent study for older children.

Researcher Mike McShane has (literally) written the book on this topic: *Hybrid Homeschooling*.[17] In explaining what parents say they like about the hybrid model, he observes:

> They feel like the traditional school schedule and calendar are out of sync with the rhythms of their family's life. But it isn't just that. Many families find themselves getting the best of homeschooling—for instance, the personalized attention, the supportive environment, more control over what is learned—and the best of traditional schooling—community, socialization, expertise, extracurriculars, and so on.[18]

The feasibility of such arrangements depends on the laws of a given state, but school and system leaders may find state policies and federal regulations more accommodating than they'd have thought. In Idaho, for instance, if homeschool students use district programming on even a part-time basis, they're included in district attendance counts for state funding. This has, not surprisingly, made it easier for districts to support homeschool families.[19] And Idaho is far from alone—at least a dozen states have similar arrangements, although the rules vary with regard to services, student eligibility, and how funding works.[20]

McShane notes that hybrid homeschooling surfaces critical questions about how schools use time, how to get parents and teachers to collaborate, and how to cultivate community.[21] The point, by now, should be clear. To a Rethinker, educational choice is less interesting as a solution than as a chance to revisit a slew of assumptions about parents, teachers, time, and schooling.

THE POSSIBILITIES OF COURSE CHOICE

In that same spirit of revisiting assumptions, it's worth touching on one other approach to educational choice—course choice. Course choice is a way to move new options into a student's current school, rather than to move a student to a new school.

While some families want to switch schools, I noted a bit earlier that more than 70 percent of parents consistently say they're satisfied with their child's school.[22] Of course, this doesn't mean those parents like *everything* about their school. They may want to stay with friends, familiar teachers, and established routines but *also* have access to alternative options, courses, curricula, or pedagogies.

Think about it this way: when you ask someone who attended college about their alma mater, there's a pretty good chance you'll tap into warm memories—and elicit enthusiastic reviews. But that may be as much about friends they made, life lessons they learned, or football games they attended as about the particulars of their education. If you ask about their freshman writing class or their big lecture course on introductory economics, you may get a very different response. That's because they're responding to specific experiences rather than the whole, happy, fuzzy package.

The same holds true in schooling, where overall satisfaction with a school doesn't necessarily reflect satisfaction with the arts program, math curriculum, reading instruction, Advanced Placement offerings, or what-have-you. Even pre-pandemic, parents who liked their school might have still grumbled about these things. Now, with so many students forcibly acclimated to a variety of remote learning options and providers, it seems only sensible that students should be able to take advantage of such options without changing schools.

Course choice allows students to tap into instructional options that aren't available at a student's school and even take courses beyond those offered by their local district. Alternative courses may be offered by neighboring districts, state higher education institutions, virtual learning providers, or specialized tutoring services. Course choice laws typically specify that the costs of enrollment are funded with a portion of the student's per-pupil outlay.

With course choice, students may be able to access courses in chemistry, constitutional law, or AP calculus even if their school lacks a chemistry teacher, a constitutional law class, or an AP math program. This can be a solution for schools dealing with staffing constraints, struggling to attract teachers in certain subjects or fields, or which have only a tiny number of students who wish to enroll in a given class.

Course choice programs can come in many flavors. New Hampshire's "Learn Everywhere" program allows high school students to earn a "certificate of credit" from any program recognized by the state board of education that can demonstrate that students have met the learning objectives. If they so choose, school districts are then empowered to recognize those credits for graduation purposes. Asked about the program's genesis, New Hampshire education commissioner Frank Edelblut offers a telling anecdote from an evening spent visiting a high school in Manchester. He recalls:

> I was greeted by a group of about 25 students all busily engaged in their FIRST Robotics Program. Some of the students were programming in JAVA to get their robot to navigate some obstacles. Others were in the shop working with two volunteer engineers from Bosch building a robot. Toward the end of my visit—it's now around 9:30—a young lady came up to me and said, "Commissioner, you've got to help us. The school closes at 10 p.m., and we need it open until 11 p.m."[23]

Edelblut says he realized that "[these kids] were going to return home at 10 or 11 at night and then do two hours of homework, because the learning they had just been engaged in for the last five hours would not count." He muses, "Somehow, we have reached a place where learning is expected to happen between 7:30 a.m. and 2:30 p.m. in a specific location."[24] His point: learning can happen at other times and in other places.

Course choice can enable and recognize that kind of learning. It allows students in a high school with a short-staffed science department to still study advanced physics. And it can make it possible for students to study robotics or Russian, even if their school lacks the requisite staff. If this all sounds pretty far removed from our heated debates about school choice, you've got the idea.

Exercise 5.3   Imagine If: What New Classes Would You Add?

Our thinking about schooling tends to be shaped by what we see and know. Thus, when we think about what new courses might be offered, who can teach them, or how they should be structured, we default to the familiar. That can be a problem. When students are no longer restricted to learning face-to-face from nearby adults, our entrenched notions of what's practical can get in our way. Today, it's no longer difficult for students to learn Korean from a linguist in Seoul or orbital dynamics from a moonlighting NASA rocket scientist. Our offerings should reflect that. This exercise works best in pairs and takes twenty-five to thirty minutes.

How It Works

Participants should be placed into pairs, with each pair imagining they've been tasked with identifying a couple of specialized new classes to be introduced into their school or system. They're not to be constrained by the current curriculum or by traditional semester- or year-long offerings. Given this kind of leeway, what classes would they choose to provide? Why these? What would make them valuable? Ask each pair to spend five minutes discussing these questions and generating a list of six classes. (Encourage pairs to think creatively and expansively: The art of making movies? The *Harry Potter* canon? The history of hip-hop? The psychology of sports? The battles of World War II? The principles of space travel? In each case, the key question should be, "Why *this* class?") Next, as a whole group, spend five to ten minutes discussing the suggestions. At this point, each pair should choose the one suggestion they find most intriguing and take five minutes to discuss three things: whether it'd be worthwhile to offer the course remotely, how long the course would need to be, and how students could demonstrate mastery of the content. Finally, as a whole group, discuss the four or five most appealing offerings and what it would take to incorporate them into the curriculum.

Takeaways

My experience is that there's far less discussion about what classes schools offer than there probably ought to be. When the topic does arise, it often defaults to the usual suspects, what there's room for in the schedule, and what school staff are prepared to teach. This exercise can be a useful way to expand that frame of reference. This also becomes a terrific opportunity to challenge our ingrained conception of what constitutes a well-rounded education.

WHAT ABOUT BAD CHOICES?

Of course, Rethinkers appreciate that we can't talk about educational choice without addressing the omnipresent concern: "What if parents make bad choices?" It's an important question. But it should be considered in context.

As we've noted, parents routinely make all manner of choices on behalf of their kids, from choosing a doctor or babysitter to managing screen time and bedtime. Parents may be imperfect choosers, but we generally trust that their judgments will be reasonable ones—and better than any practical alternative.

More to the point, there's reason to believe that parents—on the whole—actually *do* know what's best for their kids. Consider an intriguing 2021 study out of London, a city where families have long chosen their child's school (aided by expansive "league tables" that report school test performance). This study of nearly 200,000 students found that a good chunk of parents' school decisions couldn't be explained by test scores or other quantitative measures. Yet, whatever parents were focusing on instead seemed to yield *better* choices, on average, than the city's school-matching algorithm.

How'd the analysts figure that? Well, students who got their first-choice school performed better than the numbers would've predicted. When they landed in a school their parents had ranked lower, they did worse—*even when the less-preferred school's test results were statistically identical to those of the parents' first choice.*[25] In short, because parents know their kids better than anyone else, there's good reason to think they're well equipped to take into account subtle factors (about culture or curriculum) that don't show up in the numbers.

What's more, giving parents a say can help more fully engage them in their kids' education. When you limit the parental role, you disempower parents—especially parents who already feel marginalized. Several years ago, in *The School Choice Journey*, scholars Thomas Stewart and Patrick Wolf explored what happened when low-income families in Washington, DC, were awarded scholarships by the city's Opportunity Scholarship Program, allowing them to choose from a broad range of schools. At first, parents understandably focused on school safety. Only later, once that basic need was addressed and as their confidence in their judgment grew, did they start to parse academics and curricular offerings.[26]

Perhaps more telling is that Stewart and Wolf found that the act of choosing led parents to play a more active role in their schools and community. The parents in the choice program mostly had low levels of education and rarely voted or attended public meetings. Yet, after four years in the program, these same parents were out attending rallies and speaking up for their kids.[27] Giving parents a say helped spark a virtuous cycle, in which the parents grew more involved in their kids' schooling. Test scores aside, empowering parents can be a tool for engaging parents, strengthening communities, and supporting kids.

None of this is to dismiss concerns that parents may make bad choices. They certainly may, just as with day care or dentists. But we also reasonably presume that parents will make better choices when they have better information. So, how can we supply the kind of information that can help parents make good choices?

State tests and other academic assessments are one useful, consistent gauge. While such data are necessary, few parents or teachers think they're sufficient. Thus, it's crucial to consider other ways to ensure quality. There are an array of potential tools, including:

- Professional, systematic ratings of customer satisfaction, something akin to the information reported by sources like J.D. Power and Associates. These make it easy for consumers to draw on the judgments of other users.
- Scientific evaluations by credible third parties, such as those offered by *Consumer Reports*. Such objective evaluations allow experts to put new educational offerings through their paces and then score them on relevant dimensions of performance, as well as price.
- Expert evaluation of services like those provided by health inspectors (in schooling, the best-known example may be the British School Inspectorate, which inspects and reports on the quality of schools). Such evaluation focuses on examining processes and hard-to-measure outcomes, drawing on informed, subjective judgment.
- Reports reflecting user experiences—essentially, drawing on the wisdom of crowds. Online providers routinely allow users to offer detailed accounts of the good and bad they've experienced, and the public to readily view what they have to say. While these results aren't systematic or scientific, they are very good at providing context and color.

Of course, even with terrific information, parents can still make bad choices about schooling. But that's true of pretty much anyone involved in schools: teachers can make bad choices when deciding how to support a struggling student or designing an individualized education program. Administrators can make bad choices when meting out discipline or assigning a student to a teacher.

Schooling is suffused with choices. We should certainly ask what happens when a parent makes a poor choice. But we must also question the consequences of restrictive policies that limit parents' ability to find better educational options for their kids.

RETHINKING SCHOOL CHOICE

It's odd that the discussion of school choice has so often taken the shape of heated argument, given the intuitive appeal of the idea that all parents (rich and poor alike) should have a say in their kids' schooling.

Our familiar fights are both distracting and odd. Consider that in a field like health care, even those most passionate about universal, publicly funded coverage still believe that individuals should be free to choose their own doctor. In housing, even the most ardent champion of public housing thinks families should get to choose where they live. No one doubts that families should have agency when it comes to such high-stakes decisions in health care or housing. The same logic should hold in schooling. It's not selfish or risky for parents to want a say in who teaches their kids or where their kids go to school. It's normal.

It's downright weird that educational choice has focused so narrowly on students changing schools. After all, we live in an era when seemingly extraordinary options have become the norm. Consider Outschool, launched in 2016, an online platform with more than 10,000 teachers that's served over a million students. Outschool links students with experts in everything from molecular gastronomy to Hindustani classical singing.[28] Journalist Erin Schulte wrote about Outschool after her son, during the pandemic, took a ukulele class, a hip-hop dance class, a class in World War II history, and another on ninja moves.[29] Such opportunities just weren't feasible even twenty years ago.

Some Outschool teachers have taught in schools, others haven't. Teacher retention is based on feedback and student satisfaction. Teachers set their own rates, with a typical price per student of about $15 per hour. For some educators, piano teachers, translators, or professionals, this is an attractive sideline; for other teachers, it's a way to share a passion. While Outschool was designed for families with the funds to pay for enrichment opportunities, a Rethinker sees more interesting possibilities. How can these kinds of choices tap a broader pool of dynamic educators, engage and challenge more students, and expand the educational options for students and teachers?

In the end, the real promise of choice isn't just that it can help students escape struggling schools. It's that it can help make room for parents and educators alike to rethink how they want schools to work.

CHAPTER 6

A Renewed Partnership with Parents

The pandemic created a chance to rethink the relationship between home and school, between families and educators. And it's about time.

Amid extended school closures, millions of parents found that teaching was harder and more exhausting than they'd ever realized. At the same time, this abrupt window into the classroom left millions of other parents frustrated by what they saw and experienced.

During the pandemic, Baltimore City Public Schools CEO Sonja Santelises wrote a thoughtful essay for *Education Week*, observing, "I have been struck by the number of principals telling me about staff who have said they were wrong about this parent or that grandmother, now seen more as a vital ally rather than an unwanted adversary." She continued, "No longer can we dust off the welcome mats for back-to-school nights and parent-teacher conferences and then swiftly roll them back up, shooing parents away and telling them, 'Trust us.' We are now guests in their homes."[1]

For twenty years or more, such sentiments were expressed too rarely in education. Far too many parents said they felt that educators did indeed see them as adversaries or an inconvenience. Parents, fairly or not, can feel like education leaders are more absorbed in managing systems than in meeting their kids' needs. During the pandemic, for instance, parents in learning pods reported that resistance from school systems made it hard to tap crucial supports. Researchers found that learning pod families encountered "aggressive emails" and "vengeful" responses.[2] (This was similar to what many parents reported two decades ago when it came to the tutoring and public choice options of the No Child Left Behind Act.)

The data suggest that parental frustrations aren't without cause. About half of teachers report that they devote less than an hour a week to communicating with parents, guardians, and the community. Just 13 percent of teachers spend more than three hours a week doing so.[3]

Meanwhile, educators have their own grievances. When school staff reach out, their attempts to inform and engage parents can go for naught. Parent-teacher conferences can be sparsely attended. Calls home can go unanswered. Notices that get backpacked or emailed home get ignored. So the frustration cuts both ways.

Today, after years of fierce fights over school closures, masking, vaccine mandates, critical race theory, gender identity, and more, it's easy to take sides for or against parental influence. If we back away from the politics, though, almost any parent or teacher will acknowledge both that parents need to be involved and that schooling is, by its very nature, a partnership between parents and teachers.

Schools are ultimately dependent on their ability to collaborate with parents. When schools went remote, they tasked parents with providing oversight, additional explanation, tech troubleshooting, homework support, and everything else. But this was only an exaggerated version of a daily reality.

Teachers can't do it alone. School leaders need to take the lead in exploring what's needed and how to make that happen. Yet, we too rarely take the time to ask what parents need from schools and what schools need from parents.

THE HANDSHAKE BETWEEN PARENTS AND SCHOOLS

When it comes to discussing parents and parent engagement, I've found that veteran educators have learned it's safest to keep their head down, echo the company line about how much the school values parent engagement, and then deal with disengaged or troublesome parents through benign neglect.

When you get these same educators in a safe environment, however, where they feel they can speak freely, they'll voice frustration with the status quo. They'll say they'd like to do more but that they need more support from their school. They'll say that some parents don't want to be involved and that active parents aren't always helpful. And they'll say that they feel like they get blamed when students or parents aren't willing to work with them. These are all fair points. And rethinking starts with that kind of honest appraisal, not empty platitudes.

So, what should the partnership between educators and parents look like? Well, education is always a handshake between families and teachers, between students and schools.

It's a two-way street. Teachers must be professionally capable, committed to educating every child, and willing to seek ways to open a student's heart and mind. By the same token, though, the job of parents and guardians is to send children to school who are responsible, respectful, and ready to learn. This means getting their kid to school on time, making sure they do their homework, modeling personal responsibility, reading to them, and more.

Now, some readers may be uncomfortable with parts of the previous paragraph (usually the part relating to parents). That discomfort is a problem. Educators must do their part, but we can't be afraid to declare that parents have responsibilities of their own. If parents don't know how to do these things, they need mentoring. If they're unwilling to do them, they need to be challenged. And if they're unable to do them, they need support. But the answer is *not* to ignore or excuse parental inaction, and educators should have no qualms about saying so. Failing to do this isn't the empathy of an ally; it's the negligence of an enabler.

The truth is that one of the great triumphs of twenty-first-century schooling had a real (if unexpected) cost. Back in the 1980s and 1990s, it was easy to find educators who would say, "I can't teach *that* kid," and policy makers who would just shrug in response. There was a lot of attention paid to the quality of parenting and far less to the quality of schooling. Complaints that parents weren't doing their part loomed as an all-purpose excuse for educational failure. There were high-profile figures who seemed more intent on excoriating parents than on making the case that schools needed to do better.

Today, the world is very different. If educators say such things, they mutter them discreetly. It's now an accepted norm that educators should expect every child to learn. This is a seismic shift. It's been a tremendous victory and a very good thing. Period.

All that said, though, this shift has also left us disinclined to say anything that might seem to excuse educators or blame families. Today, policy makers and school leaders are reluctant to talk about whether parents are making sure their kids do their work or respect their teachers.

Even when students are routinely truant or only a handful of parents show up at parent-teacher meetings, school leaders can be reluctant to unapologetically challenge kids or parents. At a time when social-media gadflies and outrage junkies are always looking for excuses to take offense, such a challenge can feel unnerving, even risky. The result: parents aren't always clear what role they *should* play in their child's schooling, and teachers can feel like they're being treated as convenient scapegoats.

This is bad for students, educators, *and* parents. It's infantilizing. It implies that whole classes of parents are incapable of agency in their own lives or those of their children. That's not empathy. It's disrespect.

Parents, like teachers, frequently *are* overworked and overburdened. That's why it's vital to build the partnership and recalibrate mutual expectations.

Exercise 6.1   Take a Step Back: Making Sense of the Parent-Pediatrician Relationship

When it comes to health care, we hold doctors responsible for doing their job but expect patients to do their part, too. This is the implicit handshake between doctor and patient, and saying so isn't seen as blaming the patient. Things are quite different in K–12 education today, where there's often a reluctance to talk about the obligations of students and parents. This exercise draws out the comparison in order to sharpen our thinking about the competing norms. It works best in pairs and takes about twenty to twenty-five minutes.

How It Works

Organize participants into pairs and explain that the aim is to ask what it would mean if the parent-teacher relationship looked more like the parent-pediatrician relationship. (Note: the point is not that it necessarily *should* but to ask what would be different, for good and ill, if it *did*.) Ask the pairs to take five minutes to envision a parent-teacher visit and to list the responsibilities of the teacher before and after the interaction, and of the parent before and after. Then take a few minutes to have the whole group share what they listed (typically, there will be many more to-do items for teachers than parents, in both the run-up and the aftermath). After that, pairs should take another five minutes to, as best they can, think about similar responsibilities before and after a pediatric visit. (Remind students to think about the parent's role in scheduling a visit, getting their child to the doctor, getting directions for follow-up examinations or medication, and so forth.) Then have the group discuss the comparison. What do they notice? A note: there's a tendency for educators to focus on the fact that doctors seem to get more public respect than educators.

But this exercise is most useful if the group is able to focus on comparing the particulars of the parent-teacher and parent-pediatrician interaction.

Takeaways

Parents are expected to play a much more proactive role in health care than in most schools. In health care, when we say someone is a "good doctor," we generally mean that they're competent and professional; they offer a careful diagnosis and recommend the proper treatment. At that point, we expect patients and parents to assume their share of the responsibility. If a pediatrician tells a parent that their child is eating too much junk food and the parent ignores it, we don't label the physician a "bad doctor." The norms are very different in schooling. Why is that? Should the parent-teacher relationship be more like the parent-pediatrician relationship? Should we expect the pediatrician to be more responsible for what happens after the visit is over? Why or why not? Either way, what are the principles that *should* frame a healthy relationship between a professional educator and the parents of the children they teach? Such questions help us appreciate what makes for a healthy parent-school relationship but too rarely get asked.

THE TRANSPARENCY IMPERATIVE

Talk about academic transparency has taken on a more contentious tone in recent years amid a surge of legislative proposals aimed at curtailing critical race theory in classrooms. Given the context, I get why some educators may have an adverse reaction to talk of transparency. But it's probably fairer to recognize such political fights more as a *symptom* of fractured trust rather than as the *cause* of it.

Here's what I have in mind. When schools across much of the country went remote for big chunks of 2020 and 2021, parents could suddenly see what their kids were doing in school all day. It was both exhausting and illuminating. Indeed, one legacy of remote learning was the window (the transparency) it provided into schools, classrooms, and learning.

Parents got new visibility into what kids are doing, how teachers are teaching, and how schools use time. Through all of it, the thing I heard most often from parents was: "I had no idea." No idea this teacher was so organized (or disorganized). No idea their child was so adept at fractions or so confused by parts of speech. No idea how much (or how little) learning actually occurred in a school day.

Over time, routines have walled parents off from classrooms and corridors. For all the pieties about stakeholders and community, I've seen plenty of schools where parents are given the brush-off when they raise concerns about assignments or academic testing. Parenting blogs have long been filled with tirades by parents frustrated, first, by the befuddling "conceptual" approaches they encountered in trying to help their kids with math—and then by the sense that school staff didn't have time for their concerns.

When schools needed parents to get kids online, monitor their engagement, navigate balky web portals, handle lunch, supervise breaks, and serve as teacher aides, it was a stark reminder that parents aren't a nuisance but invaluable partners. At the same time, parents charged with printing out materials, managing asynchronous platforms, explaining confusing concepts, keeping their kids on task, and troubleshooting tech headaches had new appreciation for a teacher's daily burdens.

But transparency brings both costs and benefits. This isn't unique to schooling. Consider the experience of police who are increasingly required to wear body cameras. Such transparency has raised concerns about privacy and the out-of-context use of footage, even as it has also helped hold individual officers accountable (or put a quick end to unfounded allegations of misconduct). All of the same kinds of issues arise, of course, when we discuss cameras in the classroom or the merits of making instructional materials publicly available.

The Rethinker asks how to make transparency work for students, educators, and families. When is more visibility helpful in terms of instruction and parent support? When does it become unduly intrusive or disruptive? How can schools create trusting environments for tough conversations and reassure parents that they're not promoting agendas (whatever agenda that might be)? The answers aren't obvious. But asking these questions is a good way to ensure that whatever answers emerge will be useful ones.

PARENTS WANT TO KNOW THAT TEACHERS ARE THINKING ABOUT *THEIR* KID EVERY DAY

We talked in chapter 3 about the ridiculous set of tasks that teachers are expected to juggle. Thus, it's no surprise that when it comes to engaging parents, many teachers will point out (quite fairly) that their schools don't give them much time or support.

Exercise 6.2   Take a Step Back: Finding Common Ground with Parents

When I talk about the importance of bridge-building with distrustful parents, leaders will say, "Yeah, I get all that. But the trouble has been figuring out how to do it." It's a fair point, especially given the toxic state of so much public discourse today. So, practically speaking, how do you start finding common ground with parents? This exercise is intended to help prompt some fresh reflection. It works best in pairs and takes twenty to twenty-five minutes.

How It Works

Give participants five minutes to list up to a half-dozen parental complaints that they've encountered. After the whole group shares a few of those, the pairs should take another few minutes to note whether they think each complaint they've flagged is (1) understandable or (2) unreasonable. Then, as a group, discuss what distinguishes the complaints in the first bucket from those in the second. Finally, when it comes to the unreasonable complaints, the whole group should consider what questions might help provide more insight into what's driving seemingly unreasonable demands. If so inclined, it can be useful to role-play this interaction, with the facilitator acting the part of the unreasonable parent and a participant trying to clarify the underlying frustration (I suggest the facilitator play the part with the presumption that there actually *is* some understandable—even sympathetic—motivation, as that's both true to life and best illustrates the value of taking time to listen and learn).

Takeaways

Especially for leaders who are busy running schools or systems, it's easy to get in the habit of regarding parental complaints as just one more fire to be doused. That's understandable. But it means that root causes go unexplored and instructive signals can be missed. Taking the time to assess the merits of parent complaints, away from the heat of the moment, can spark frank discussion about which complaints contain important warning signs. Asking questions that clarify what's driving seemingly frivolous complaints can be a tool both for better addressing potential problems and for making those parents feel valued and heard.

During the pandemic, when I spoke with learning pod parents, a recurrent theme was how much many of them liked getting daily feedback on how their kid did that day. A huge number of parents told me that wasn't what they were used to.

While some might choose to read this as a critique of teachers, I don't think that's right. It's really a reflection of how we've set up schools. Communicating with families just isn't central to the day-to-day routine of most schools. It's typically a "this too" that gets raised *after* schedules are arranged, classrooms are staffed, materials are procured, and assessments are administered.

Consider a teacher's daily routine. They get to school at a designated time, frequently *well* before the start of the official school day. They then spend the day instructing classes (without bathroom breaks), monitoring students, prepping lessons, and sometimes subbing for absent colleagues. Asked about communicating with parents, teachers will say that, at best, they'll have a moment to thumb off a text or a ClassDojo message while monitoring lunch or hurrying to the restroom between classes, and that the only obvious time to make a call is while driving home.

Professional days are mostly reserved for trainings or curriculum planning. Then the school year ends and teachers are off the clock until mid-August. Most schools make no deliberate attempt to build—into the school day, week, or year—a window for sustained interaction with parents. School leaders tend to provide little guidance on how such interaction should unfold and voice no explicit expectation for how often it should happen.

High school teachers, charged with the most disengaged kids, routinely have a load that can approach 150 students a day. Keeping up with that many students, let alone their parents, can be overwhelming. A teacher intent on speaking to each student's parents once a month is signing up for about thirty-five conversations a week—that's seven every day. Even if each call takes only five to ten minutes, that's an hour every day (before accounting for time spent scheduling calls, rescheduling missed calls, or dealing with language issues). And, when you consider that middle and high schoolers may have a half-dozen teachers, it's safe to say few parents would *want* that many calls.

Worse, partly because parents aren't used to schools reaching out, even when teachers make extraordinary efforts, parents can be unresponsive, unsure of what they need, or even confrontational. A few years ago, I worked with a school that was all in on finding ways to connect with parents. Staff ran an extensive planning process and devised an ambitious strategy to stagger parent-teacher meeting times, add translators, provide transportation, and so forth. And the result was . . . dismal. They saw only the barest of upticks in parent responses or attendance. The staff was discouraged, feeling like they'd wasted a lot of time and energy. So, it's easy to understand why some educators may have mixed feelings about trying to engage parents.

And yet, when doubts about the utility of all this start to creep in, keep in mind that parent involvement matters *a lot* for student success. A 2017 study of 11,000 households analyzed schools that simply sent parents a half-dozen reminders about the importance of student attendance during the year.[4] The result: an 8 percent reduction in absences and an even bigger drop in chronic absenteeism.

A study of Title I elementary schools found that face-to-face parent-teacher meetings, sending materials home, and regular phone check-ins substantially boosted academic performance among low-income students.[5] The National Coalition for Parent Involvement in Education has surveyed the research and concluded that "no matter their income or background, students with involved parents are more likely to have higher grades and test scores, attend school regularly, [and] have better social skills."[6] Makes sense.

EVERY CHILD, EVERY DAY

I know, I know. At this point in a conversation, every school leader tells me that they're already working to engage families but that it's easier said than done. They're right, of course. Then they inevitably ask, "You have any better suggestions?" Well, I don't. But I know some people who do.

In Arizona's Phoenix Union High School District, Superintendent Chad Gestson had an intriguing response when schools went remote in March 2020. Worried that the district's 30,000 high schoolers were going to fall off the radar (as happened to something like one in five students across the land), he announced that school staff would be connecting with "every student, every day."

With schools shuttered and staff working from home, Gestson reminded employees that everyone was still on the clock and said that every district employee—teachers, support staff, and administrators (including him)—would take about ten students and check in every day.

The exercise surfaced all manner of challenges. For one thing, it turned out that a huge chunk of the district's contact numbers were inaccurate. Gestson recalls that, at first, he had working phone numbers for just four of his ten students. "Those first few days were spent trying backup numbers, calling aunts or other family members, and just trying to make sure we knew how to find our students," he says. The early calls mostly dealt with technical issues related to remote learning, but they soon evolved to focus on how students and families were faring. Gestson says, "Sometimes we'd talk to the student every day. In other families, the parent said, 'Call me instead [of my child].'" Staff just followed the family's lead.

Gestson says that, beyond strengthening the bond with families, the calls also surfaced useful insights. "One thing we learned was that a lot of students had strong relationships [with school staff]. Kids would tell us, 'I just talked to my math teacher or that coach.' We also learned which students didn't have those relationships. We heard about families struggling with food or housing and could refer them to community support."

The district stitched together software that enabled staff to more readily steer all students to someone who could assist them. By fall 2020, Phoenix had ended the daily calls but adopted a referral-for-intervention approach in which any staff member can flag the same kinds of issues that surfaced on the calls, with 10,000 such requests for assistance filed during the 2021–2022 school year.

Of course, Gestson was hardly the only leader to rethink parent engagement during the pandemic. The Canopy project has sought to collect some of the more promising ways that schools responded to COVID-19.[7] At New York City's Concourse Village Elementary School, prior to COVID-19, communication with families was sporadic and the principal thought families liked it that way. During the pandemic, though, the school began a weekly check-in—as in Phoenix, these first focused on remote learning, then gradually evolved. These check-ins surfaced pent-up parent interest, which the school built on with monthly surveys, follow-up phone calls, and virtual visits.

At Uxbridge High School, in Massachusetts, the leadership team instituted regular, individualized conferences with counselors, teachers, and families to support struggling students. At Urban Assembly Maker Academy in New York, the assistant principal and selected staff would spend three Fridays a month knocking on doors to reconnect with kids who had stopped logging on or engaging.[8]

Such measures are heartening. But a Rethinker can't help but wonder why they're the exception and not the rule. Why wasn't all of this being done before the pandemic? Why are these practices so unusual that the Canopy project would flag these schools as innovators? And why are these efforts so often reserved for struggling kids, rather than for every student? These are questions that deserve careful thought and serious answers.

Exercise 6.3 Imagine If: A Guide for Interacting with Parents

Watching school leaders grapple with engagement can be revealing just because they'll realize the number of possible measures they haven't really explored. This exercise asks participants to operate as a task force charged with creating a guide for parent-teacher interaction. It works best in small groups and takes forty-five minutes to an hour, though it also works well as a project pursued over a more extended time frame.

How It Works

The small groups have been deputized to devise new guidelines governing parent outreach for their school or system. Groups should start, of course, by asking what problem(s) they're trying to solve. Give each group five minutes to address this question and then share some of the responses with the whole group. Next, each group should develop its guidelines across four dimensions:

- **Frequency of interaction:** How often should teachers be expected to talk to parents? How often should *some* member of the school staff be checking in with families?
- **Depth of interaction:** How substantial and extensive should interactions be? What kinds of activities and formats are useful and appropriate?
- **Context of interaction:** What circumstances make for a comfortable, trusting exchange? What norms should govern the preparation and scheduling of outreach?
- **Mode of interaction:** What constitutes an interaction? Should one-way communications (like unanswered email or texts) count? How personal should interactions be (are calls or video chats, for instance, as good as in-person sit-downs)?

Give each group ten minutes to develop a three-sentence vision for each of the four dimensions, with a concrete example for each. Then ask the groups to take another fifteen minutes to sketch out the activities required to translate the principles into practice. Finally, ask each small group to take three minutes to present its approach to the group—and then have the whole group discuss what changes are necessary to make any of this possible.

Takeaways

When it comes to parent engagement, educators repeatedly tell me, "We just don't get much opportunity to really dig into this." That's not a surprise. If you peruse teacher preparation coursework, PD workshops, or conference programs, you just don't see much attention to interacting with parents. So there's a need for time to think about how to engage parents and signal that doing so is important. I find that many educators initially struggle with this exercise. Let them know that's okay. There's great value simply in reminding educators that their relationship with parents is not a given but something over which they can exert enormous influence.

PRACTICAL STRATEGIES FOR ENGAGING FAMILIES

If you want some more thoughts on how to get started on the parent piece, it's worth checking out the work of Harvard University's Karen Mapp. She's been elbow-deep in parent engagement for more than two decades and is a fount of practical advice. She's written books like *Beyond the Bake Sale: The Essential Guide to Family-School Partnerships* and helped launch the District Leaders Network on Family and Community Engagement. She's flagged a number of good places to dig in when it comes to rethinking the parent-school relationship.

Get a Better Picture of Parent Engagement

Oddly, as much as school leaders talk about the value of both data and engaging parents, many schools have little reliable information on where things stand with parent engagement. To help with that, Mapp has created a free forty-one-question survey that school officials can download. She urges administrators to form a team of parents, community members, teachers, and students to distribute the survey to parents—either online, by hand, or both. The results can illuminate existing relationships, spotlight needs, and suggest next steps.[9]

Bolster Parent-Teacher Interaction

Arizona's Creighton School District has sought to embed parent engagement in a broader network by having each family participate in three teacher-hosted, seventy-five-minute small group meetings during the school year. At the meetings, teachers walk parents through student performance data in simple, bar-graph formats. This not only gives parents the chance to see how their child is doing but gives them the opportunity to meet other parents, discuss student performance with them, and develop more connections to the school community. (This matters most for parents who may otherwise feel like they're on the outside looking in.) Parents and teachers collectively set academic goals for the next sixty days, and then revisit those at each meeting.[10]

Create School Materials with Parents in Mind

The program Teachers Involve Parents in Schoolwork advises teachers to create homework that includes tips for parents on how best to assist and that also requires students to talk to their parents about their assignments. Don't *just* encourage parents to help with homework; the point is to give students homework that invites parental input and tells parents *how* they can help. Mapp suggests soliciting ideas from parents as to what they'd find useful and then including relevant advice and discussion in school communications.[11]

Build a Parent Education Program

The Parent University at Boston Public Schools offers classes for parents and family members on a variety of topics, all linked to the district's learning outcomes.[12] In every course, even a cooking class, parents are taught skills that equip them to support their kids academically. School leaders are able to reach out to Parent University, which hosts its classes at schools or community centers when they see a need on campus. Staffing is mostly provided by external community organizations.[13]

None of this is rocket science, much less a cure-all. But it's sensible. It can help. And it's well worth exploring.

IT'S WHO YOU KNOW

Kids benefit from access to a wide range of mentors, role models, and supportive adults. But finding ways to provide that within the conventional schoolhouse can be a heavy lift.

It's tougher still because digital life and pandemic-inspired habits have compounded the "bowling alone" phenomenon first identified by Harvard professor Robert Putnam in the 1990s. Putnam noted, across an array of measures, that Americans were joining fewer groups and spending more time in solo activities than they used to (hence, the title of his influential book, *Bowling Alone*).[14]

Today, kids are enmeshed in fewer social networks than ever before. They are far less likely than they once were to engage in things like church groups, the Boy Scouts, and 4-H clubs. As a result, they encounter fewer potential mentors, which matters for everything from learning to college admissions to landing a job (since about half of all jobs come through personal relationships).[15]

This shift matters more for children with fewer advantages because, as Putnam has observed in *Our Kids*, networks of college-educated parents tend to include many more people with "social influence" (like politicians, CEOs, and professors) than do those of the less educated.[16] Indeed, celebrated economist Raj Chetty has found that connections to the affluent significantly increases the economic mobility of low-income children.[17]

A big obstacle is that mentoring has historically been limited by where people live and who happens to reside in that community. Low-income families are just less likely to live down the block or casually mingle with networked professionals. That can make it tough for kids in low-income communities to forge connections with affluent mentors. New tools can help do something about that.

In their book *Who You Know*, Julia Freeland Fisher and Daniel Fisher explore how schools can expand students' access to relationships that might otherwise be out of reach, noting that students can now hear virtually from a range of adults about a wide variety of jobs.[18] In a world full of active retirees, remote workers, and the self-employed, it's easier to find adults with the flexibility to engage and the time and interest to serve as mentors.

As Julia Freeland Fisher has put it, "Whom you know matters and what you know matters, but especially powerful is *who knows you know what you know.*" Recommendations from those with clout or connections carry added weight, especially for kids with fewer advantages. As Freeland Fisher explains, the power of credentialed mentors is that they're "invested in, and bear witness to, students' strengths and abilities," enabling them to "vouch for them down the line."[19]

Expanded mentoring may be appealing in theory but, of course, it gets more complicated in practice. It can be daunting to vet participants, form a network of willing mentors, coordinate times and schedules, police the process, and do everything else that's necessary. Fortunately, school systems are well positioned to manage these tasks—and they can find help.

School systems don't need to build any of this from scratch. Rather, they can partner with platforms like CommunityShare or ImBlaze that streamline the act of locating experts and potential partners. Tucson-based CommunityShare, which exclusively serves Arizona schools, has been used by more than 11,000 teachers to locate community members who can speak to particular topics or lessons. ImBlaze, which works with more than a hundred schools across the country, links students with local internship opportunities and provides a reporting system that allows employers and schools to monitor hours, submit required reports, and share essential information regarding openings and experiences.

The benefits are intuitive for anyone who's ever seen the right coach or counselor prompt a kid to discover a new passion. Connecting students to professionals, mentors, and the well-off can benefit all kids, of course, but especially those less likely to make those connections outside school. While none of this is easy, schools today can readily stream experts and mentors into classrooms or advisories—something that would've been impractical even a decade ago.

DRIVER'S ED AND DIGITAL DEVICES

Helping kids navigate the world of social media is one place where schools and parents sorely need each other. As we discussed in chapter 4, today's tweens and teens spend a staggering amount of time online. That creates the need for new kinds of collaboration between parents and schools. When a student is cyberbullied by a classmate or engages in alarming online behavior, it's essential that families and teachers work together to respond. Today, too often, that's not how it works.

Every technology brings both good and bad. That was the rationale for introducing driver's education last century, at a time when driving became a rite of passage and cars were the most powerful technology a student would encounter. Schools tapped their institutional muscle and instructional acumen to support parents who lacked the time, know-how, or temperament to teach students how to harness this dangerous tool.

However much we may deride driver's education today, it's a pretty good model for thinking about kids in the digital world. As experience and research make clear, a tween's phone should be regarded not as a colorful bauble but a powerful piece of equipment that needs to be handled responsibly. Unfortunately, in many schools and homes today, the coaching that youth get on how to handle social media looks a lot like tossing a twelve-year-old the keys to a Harley and saying, "Hey, remember to drive safely. Oh, and please stay away from the biker bars."

That's not good enough. As Yuval Levin, author of *A Time to Build*, has observed, "If Instagram and TikTok were brick-and-mortar spaces in your neighborhood, you probably would never let even your teenager go to them alone. Parents should have the same say over their children's presence in these virtual spaces." While federal statute stipulates that children under thirteen aren't even supposed to have social-media accounts without parental consent, Levin noted, the law is routinely ignored.[20]

Tweens and teens are going to have devices. They need them to access class materials, arrange rides home, listen to music, take pictures, pay for things, talk to their friends, and much else. Odds are, kids are going to use these devices both at home and in school.[21] Helping them learn to do so safely and responsibly can't be solely the province of either parents or educators.

Parents need to set boundaries and model responsible behavior. Schools can complement and inform those efforts by coaching parents who want help, sharing healthy practices, and teaching students to navigate the perils of life online. It has to be a partnership. What exactly should that partnership look like and how should it work? That's fertile ground for a Rethinker.

RETHINKING THE PARTNERSHIP WITH PARENTS

As students have experienced an epidemic of learning loss, emotional trauma, and social isolation, parents have made it clear that they're looking for help. This offers educators the opportunity to strike a new deal with parents, one anchored by shared norms and sensible expectations.

Striking that deal requires that school and system leaders see parents as partners. That means coaching them. It means keeping parents apprised of what's happening in school and asking how things are going at home. It means making it easy for parents to see what's being taught and what materials are being used. It means valuing parental concerns and making clear that parental input is getting heard—even (or especially) when it's not being adopted.

When discussing how to more fruitfully think about the parent-teacher partnership, I sometimes tell the story of a visit with the director of an urban literacy program who helped me understand why some parents don't read to their kids (or why it doesn't help as much as we might expect). Here's how I related it in *Letters to a Young Education Reformer*:

> "Rick," he said, "the stuff we take for granted would really blow your mind. I remember this one father. He was a high school dropout and working a

tough job, but he was doing what we tell them. He was making the time. He had his infant on his lap and was reading. But he didn't have that picture of 'reading to a kid' that you and I take for granted."

"How do you mean?" I asked.

"He was reading, but it wasn't what we usually think of as reading to an infant. It was like he was reading the paper. He wasn't varying his voice or using inflection. He wasn't pointing to pictures. He was intent on reading every word before turning the page. He had the kid planted awkwardly on his knee, and neither of them looked comfortable."

He said, "We worked with the dad on all that. Showed him how to position the kid more comfortably. Had him point out pictures, change up his voice, and have more fun with it. That's all it really took. The next month, it was a different story."[22]

That's the kind of family-school partnership that can make a big difference for kids. It's not about casting blame. It's about educators and parents helping each other do better.

In an age of information overload, expanding options, and social fragmentation, local school systems have a crucial role to play as trusted hubs of mentoring, coaching, access, and information. For parents who don't know how to read to their kid, school systems can be curators of instructional videos and a go-to for finding coaching programs. For parents seeking a tutor, learning pod, or summer enrichment program, schools can be conduits to an array of high-quality options. For all parents, school systems should be a fount of reliable data, support, and advice.

Put another way, the local school system's relationship with parents should evolve from the factory-era role of being *the* purveyor of schooling to one where staff wield their expertise and institutional assets to better meet the varied needs of students and families.

This requires that education leaders win the trust of educators *and* parents. Build those relationships from day one. Make it a priority. Reach out to civic leaders and invite them to school. Regularly ask parents and teachers about their concerns. Give parents a window into what's happening in classrooms. Teach staff that parents and guardians (even when they're disputing a decision or choosing a nontraditional option) should be viewed as partners rather than adversaries. Rethinkers suspect that leaders who make the time to do this will find it well worth the trouble.

CHAPTER 7

A New Public School Tradition?

I n *Anna Karenina*, Leo Tolstoy famously observed, "All happy families are alike; each unhappy family is unhappy in its own way."

I'm not sure whether Tolstoy was right about families. When it comes to schools, though, I've often thought it's the other way around. Good schools differ in all kinds of ways. Some feature hard-nosed discipline and others a let-it-be kind of culture. Some are intently focused on math and science, others on the arts. Some embrace technology, others don't. Some are staffed by energetic youngsters, others by grizzled veterans.

When it comes to bad schools, though, there's a kind of dreary uniformity. Classrooms manage to be both disorganized and oddly rote. Teachers may cover the required material, but with little student interest or attention. Lessons are lackluster and the air reeks of lifeless obligation. Classrooms may be chaotic or they may be passive, but they're consistently devoid of wonder or passion.

Nearly four decades ago, in *Horace's Compromise*, Theodore Sizer aptly described classrooms shaped by a comfortable but dysfunctional agreement: the teacher would pretend to teach, and the students would pretend to learn. The result was a pageant of schooling shorn of the substance of learning.[1]

I'm skeptical that there's a single recipe for unwinding Horace's compromise or creating a good school, but I'm firmly convinced that there are many ways to get there. Rethinkers believe that all of these paths start by asking practical questions, embracing the sacred promise of public education, and freeing educators and families from the heavy hand of convention. I hope this volume can help with that.

After all, as I noted a decade ago in *Cage-Busting Leadership*, education leaders can find it tough to make even modest changes. They are stymied by a sense that their hands are tied—even when they're not. The thick web of rules, regulations, contracts, funding requirements, and routines create the sense of omnipresent obstacles. This has fostered a weird cultural schism, with advocates and academics urging innovation from the sidelines, while school and system leaders feel like they're obliged to operate within a constricting cage.[2] The upshot is that we mustn't excuse comfortable inertia but neither should we urge leaders to embrace frenzied, incoherent, or scattershot agendas.

In that spirit, there are four things I want to touch upon in this closing chapter. First, I want to be very clear about why rethinking is wholly consistent with a commitment to public education. Second, I want to offer a few guardrails that can ensure rethinking isn't any harder than it needs to be. Third, knowing that some readers may wonder how to get started, I'll offer a few suggestions. Finally, I want to offer a few words on the kind of leadership it takes if rethinking is to amount to more than idle chatter.

ANOTHER WAY TO THINK ABOUT PUBLIC EDUCATION

I learned long ago that the kinds of rethinking I've sketched in this volume can be interpreted by some as an "attack" on public education. They are troubled by talk of reconceiving the teacher's job or embracing the possibilities of educational choice. I want to take a moment to directly address these concerns.

First off, no one should imagine that defending public education means protecting or preserving every element of the apparatus as it currently exists. Indeed, one of the best ways to defend public education is to ensure that it's meeting the needs of families and communities.

For this reason, over the past century and a half, public school reformers have promoted compulsory attendance, district consolidation, larger schools, smaller schools, home economics, vocational education, standardized testing, forced busing, magnet schools, merit pay, tracking, detracking, and much else. Some of these ideas were good. Some weren't. But none of them were an "attack" on public education—they were measures intended to improve public schooling.

Public education can encompass a lot of approaches, and it can be organized in a lot of different ways. Rather than insist that defending it requires staffing schools or structuring choices like we did in the 1970s (or the 1920s), we better serve its aims by allowing ourselves to rethink its particulars and then consider potential changes on their merits.

Indeed, the pandemic reminded us that there are lots of ways to deliver schooling—as when months of mandatory homeschooling and remote teaching were casually deemed to be self-evidently "public."

Rethinking asks that we allow ourselves to explore what amounts to a "new public school tradition," one that is committed to public education's historic aims but open to a range of assumptions about how schools go about their work, provide options, and engage with families. (I'm hardly the first to suggest the value of this kind of rethinking. More than four decades ago, the iconic sociologist James Coleman argued that we would do well to occasionally reappraise our judgment as to what constitutes public schooling in light of broader social, economic, and cultural shifts.[3] And historian Ashley Berner's book *No One Way to School* offers a terrific overview of the philosophical and practical issues at work.[4])

Admittedly, a number of the ideas we've touched upon might stretch our traditional notions of public education, challenge familiar rules, or involve educators and organizations that reside outside the bounds of public school systems. But it's not clear why that should be particularly disconcerting. After all, when viewed closely, the hard-and-fast lines often used to denote "public" are a good deal blurrier than we pretend.

Keep in mind that public education is already rife with private activity. State departments of education and local school districts contract with for-profit firms for books, buses, information systems, textbooks, testing, computers, counseling programs, and so much else. Yet we tend to casually regard all this as obviously public, mostly because we're used to it. The point is simply that there's nothing especially novel about using private partners to provide mentoring, microschools, or math instruction.

There are many legitimate ways to serve public ends. For instance, public school systems charge fees for various extracurricular activities, raise funds from raffles, collect PTA contributions, and accept funds from private philanthropy. Heck, many public systems also place some hard-to-serve students with special needs in private placements, paying for the services with public dollars. Does this mean such systems should no longer be regarded as public? Hardly anyone suggests that. The point is that public education turns out to be a broader, more capacious designation than ideologues might allow.

It's often suggested that public schools are public because they're funded by tax dollars (e.g., public funds). Of course, in states where the elected legislature decides to introduce voucher programs, course choice programs, or charter schools, they're democratically deciding to fund those services with public dollars. That means that, if we take the public-dollars criteria seriously, such programs certainly qualify as public. Indeed, strictly applied, the public-dollars criteria yield a pretty expansive sense of public education. And that's okay.

Perhaps more importantly, simply calling something "public" doesn't mean it necessarily serves happy ends. In common usage, the phrase "public schooling" is suffused with vague, happy notions of inclusivity and fairness. But "public" isn't a magic word. Don't take it from me: take it from public education's staunchest defenders.

After all, many who celebrate public education will, in the next breath, lament that these schools are underfunded, segregated, oppressive, engaged in discriminatory discipline, or obsessed with testing and sorting kids. Many who champion democratic control will also assert that a given decision is undemocratic if they believe elected officials got it wrong (as with recent controversies regarding how schools teach issues of race or gender). In practice, these things are complicated, contingent, and subjective, and simply calling a school "public" doesn't change that.

What's my point? Believe me, it's *not* to play word games about "public." It's to note that things are less clear-cut than defenders of the status quo are prone to acknowledge. A Rethinker tends to believe there are lots of ways to provide and serve the aims of public education. To borrow a bit of Silicon Valley–speak: Rethinkers see that pluralism as a feature, not a bug, of the American system.

We should be open to the possibility that approaches sometimes regarded as less public might actually offer *better* avenues to fulfilling public goals. Take the promotion of citizenship and democratic participation as an example. University of Arkansas professor Patrick Wolf has examined the evidence and found that private schools might actually do a *better* job at preparing citizens. Across more than eighty findings, Wolf finds that, after controlling for relevant student characteristics, private schools dramatically outperform public schools in fostering student tolerance, democratic participation, civic knowledge, and voluntarism. (If you're wondering why that might be, a leading hypothesis is that private schools find it *easier* to teach democratic values because they've a clearer sense of mission, more trust, and are less hamstrung by political considerations.)[5]

A commitment to public schooling requires holding fast to the core principles of universalizing opportunity and serving the community, but also freeing ourselves from the diktats of ideology and historic happenstance as we do so. In an age when social and technological changes have created extraordinary new challenges and possibilities, pinched renderings of public schooling are untenable and counterproductive. They stymie our thinking and divert attention from critical questions. A more expansive conception is truer to our traditions and better suited to the work ahead.

DON'T MAKE THIS HARDER THAN IT HAS TO BE

Once you embrace the rethinking mind-set and start asking why things work the way they do, more and more questions suggest themselves. This can quickly get unwieldy, even overwhelming. And it can defeat the whole purpose of rethinking. Instead of a practical effort to solve pressing problems for students, families, and teachers, Rethinkers can wind up overwhelmed by the sheer number of possibilities.

How do we steer clear of this trap? Well, here are four principles that can help.

You Don't Need to Change Everything

We spoke about "Chesterton's fence" in chapter 1, and the idea that we shouldn't change things until we understand why they look the way they do. Put another way, change for change's sake is *not* the goal. In fact, Chesterton's key insight was that old things can be old *because* they work, and we shouldn't change them until we're confident that they've stopped working or that we've got a better solution. Rethinkers are obliged to make the case that changes to school schedules, staffing, assessment, or what-have-you aren't just new fads more likely to breed disruption and disappointment. That caution can help keep the focus on what matters most.

Focus on What You Can Change

One of the defining characteristics of a gripe session is the tendency to focus on things that we *can't* change. When parents, teachers, or administrators start voicing frustration with the state testing schedule or fuming about new graduation requirements, it's usually a case of blowing off steam about things that are beyond their control. Rethinkers seek to concentrate on the things that they *can* change. (Generally speaking, this is a good rule of thumb for minimizing frustration and maximizing impact.) And, I've long found that once you're looking at things with an eye to what you *can* change, there's much more opportunity for movement than you might imagine.[6]

Focus on What It Takes to Make Change Actually Happen

One way to distinguish between blue-sky thinking and practice-oriented rethinking is by asking, "What would it take for this change to actually happen?" The better your answer, the better the idea. Here's what I mean: there's an iconic episode of the TV show *South Park* in which gnomes are busy stealing the town's underpants. Why are they doing this? Well, the gnomes have a three-part plan.

Phase 1: Steal underpants.
Phase 2: ???
Phase 3: Get rich.

As the gnomes eventually realized, there's something missing there. It's whether we know what happens in phase two that determines whether our blue-sky thinking is a self-indulgent distraction or something more.

Focus on the Practical Challenges That Can Get in Your Way

Over the decades, one of my great frustrations with would-be education reformers has been their habit of responding to disappointment by saying, "Whoops! We had an unexpected implementation problem." The Rethinker's job is to *anticipate* the problems that can get in the way. As far as a Rethinker is concerned, there's *no such thing* as an "implementation problem." What matters in schooling is what actually happens to students and educators. That's *all* implementation. Calling something an "implementation problem" is just a fancy way of saying we didn't think things through beforehand. Contemplating the obstacles can help avoid the temptation to bite off more than you can chew.

All this can probably be summarized as: take a deep breath, think before you act, and focus on getting a given change right. Resist the urge to rethink everything, everywhere, all at once. Instead, focus on what's important, what's feasible, what change requires, and what can get in your way. That's how Rethinkers ensure this work isn't any harder than it needs to be.

GETTING STARTED

If you've made it this far, you may be wondering how to get started. At the outset, I noted that this wouldn't be a book of prescriptions. If you didn't believe me back in the beginning, I trust you do by now.

Our project hasn't been to compile a to-do list of what *must* be done in your school or system but to help you consider what *might* be done. And those answers will look different depending on your students, educators, and community. All that said, even in the most patient of audiences, someone inevitably says: "Okay. But given all that, where would you suggest getting started?"

It's a fair question. For one thing, this is what the exercises are for and why they're designed for groups. You get started not by thinking big thoughts but by gathering a group of colleagues, staff, or partners, and starting to ask questions together. But I know that's not a satisfying response. So, as a general proposition, here are the half-dozen places where I'd be inclined to start.

Know Where Time Goes

I'm always surprised at the little we know about how students and educators actually spend their time. The fact that the Columbia time diary study or the Providence disruption study are so novel should be a blaring wake-up call for educators and researchers alike. We need to know much more about how time is used, how much time teachers spend on things that matter, and where time is being frittered away on things that are unproductive. How much time do students actually spend learning in school? How much time do they spend learning outside the schoolhouse? What are teachers doing that they shouldn't or that causes students to tune out? These are questions that demand answers.

Figure Out Whether New Tech Tools Are Actually Going to Be Useful

Instead of looking at education technology like a hacker ("Is this impressive?"), think of it the same way most of us do our cellphones ("Is it useful?"). What matters is whether new tools make it easier to teach, mentor, or support students. Too much impressive-seeming technology winds up complicating the lives of educators by creating new headaches, distractions, and data-entering requirements. When it comes to gauging the promise of new technology, ask: How does this *actually* work? What will it take for this technology to deliver for students? What has to change for that to happen? What could go wrong? If the answers don't satisfy, neither will the technology.

Crack the Chicken-and-Egg Staffing Dilemma

Schools can't rethink what teachers do unless educators are prepared for new roles and compensated for new responsibilities, but it makes no sense to train people for roles that don't exist. Getting unstuck requires partnerships between select training programs and school systems, along with opportunities for schools to operate outside familiar licensure requirements, job descriptions, and salary schedules. This is an argument for local educators and community leaders to exploit all the freedom they may already possess, rather than wait upon grand policy fixes to be worked out in Washington, DC, or state capitals.

Make Educational Choice Work for Everyone

School choice is frequently approached as a moralistic debate. A Rethinker, though, is less interested in arguing *whether* policy makers should give families more educational options than in exploring the practical possibilities and challenges of doing so. For students bored or bullied in traditional classrooms, can hybrid homeschooling offer a promising alternative? For disengaged high schoolers, can course choice provide access to a richer educational experience? What supports, information, and tools do families need to take advantage of such options? Remember that the one-size-fits-all schoolhouse was less a conscious choice than a concession to the constraints of an earlier era. How might evolving options help better meet the diverse needs of students, families, and educators in this one?

Treat Parents Like Partners

Schools need to renew their partnership with parents. This means investing far more energy in reaching out to parents and engaging them in their child's education. It *also* means being clear about expectations and parent responsibilities. In other words, treat parents like real partners. Educators should ask what it would take to regularly check in with parents by phone, text, or home visit and explore the implications of that expanded interaction. Schools should establish opportunities for parents to give input while reexamining parent-teacher collaboration around homework and digital devices. In an age of information overload, school leaders would do well to ask how they might serve as a hub of good options and a source of trusted information.

Don't Reinvent the Wheel

One of the odder sights of the pandemic was watching so many of the nation's 14,000 public school districts each try to stitch together a home-grown remote-learning system. It proved exhausting for district staff, overwhelming for teachers, and a payday for consultants. It doesn't make much sense for so many districts—which have a lot on their plates but not a lot of tech savants on payroll—to knock themselves out starting up a virtual service that could easily be imported from Silicon Valley or Sri Lanka. School systems should instead partner with specialized providers to offer virtual options that families can access inside or outside school.

Exercise 7.1   Imagine If: Getting Started

Rethinking isn't an academic exercise, it's a practical one. Too often, talk of school reform can feel abstract and aspirational, focused on sweeping calls for innovation rather than on how tools, talent, time, or options might be used to answer a specific challenge. This exercise is intended to help with that. It works best in pairs and takes twenty to twenty-five minutes.

How It Works

Pairs should take five minutes to identify three specific challenges they see in their school or system. Encourage participants to hold off on offering solutions or innovations and stay focused on the problems themselves. Participants need to keep asking one another: What's the problem? How do you know it's a problem? How big a problem is it? Next, have pairs take five to ten minutes to select one problem they've flagged, consider strategies that might address it, and *how* each might help. Then, give the pairs five minutes to select one strategy and focus on what it would take for it to work. Finally, have pairs share out their problem, the suggested response, and their biggest concern regarding feasibility.

Takeaways

Many of the examples and ideas we've discussed can strike educators as too far afield from the day-to-day to be practical. The point is to start with specific challenges participants face in their school or system and then discuss solutions designed to address *that*. It's a good reminder that Rethinkers embrace deliberation and precision and need to resist the "fire, ready, aim" mind-set so prevalent in schooling.

THE CASE OF TUTORING

To get going, it can help to consider how the rethinking lens might apply to a particular improvement strategy. Pandemic learning loss, for instance, put a bright spotlight on the promise of tutoring. States and school systems launched ambitious tutoring initiatives.

In theory, the promise of tutoring is obvious. It means more individualized attention, geared to a student's real-time needs. And there's evidence that tutoring can deliver. A systematic survey of gold-standard studies has found that a year of tutoring consistently adds months of academic progress—especially in the early grades.[7] Another review, of nearly two hundred high-quality studies, concluded that "high-dosage tutoring" (at least eighty to ninety minutes of weekly tutoring for thirty-six weeks) is one of the few school-based interventions with big benefits for both reading and math.[8]

So, the appeal of tutoring is clear. However, as powerful as tutoring may be in theory, it can be expensive and logistically difficult in practice. Several years ago, the Houston school district launched Apollo 20, an ambitious tutoring experiment for students in grades 5 and 9 in a targeted set of middle and high schools.

The effort, for two grade levels of students in a limited number of schools, was backed by millions in start-up funding and intensive hands-on support from a research team at Harvard University. Despite all these advantages, the practical challenges of recruiting, training, and retaining enough part-time tutors proved daunting. The idea was a good one, but ultimately too difficult and too costly to operate at the desired scale.

That's where rethinking can help. For starters, it's critical to get clear on the problem tutoring is intended to solve. Is it providing more demonstration, practice, and feedback at particular tasks (like math operations or essay writing)? Is it coaching on behavior and study skills? Is it providing a connection to a caring adult who will offer support and encouragement? Is it low-level remediation or, perhaps, support with high-level concepts?

It frequently gets lost in the mix, *but the answers to these questions matter.* Providing students with real-time assistance on math operations is different from giving them a personal relationship with a mentor. An extended face-to-face session is very different from a brief, text-based virtual interaction.

Yet proposals for tutoring interventions tend to make little allowance for what's actually needed or what tutors are equipped to do. Rather, states scramble to create rosters of tutors, districts urgently create loosely defined tutoring programs on the fly, and no one has too much time to worry about the details.

What's a better approach? Let's start with what we know about how tutoring works. Scholars at Brown University's Annenberg Institute have studied this closely and offered several sensible design principles for effective tutoring.[9]

The first relates to *frequency*: research suggests the value of high doses, featuring at least three sessions a week or intensive, weeklong, small-group programs. Students in K–5 may benefit more from shorter, more frequent sessions (say five twenty-minute sessions a week).

The second relates to *group size*: tutoring needn't be one-on-one. The research suggests that tutors can work effectively with three to four students at a time before it starts to feel less personalized and more like small group instruction.

The third is a matter of *scheduling*: the evidence suggests that tutoring conducted during the school day leads to larger learning gains than that delivered after school or during the summer.

A fourth has to do with *staffing*: tutoring is distinct enough from classroom teaching that formal teaching experience appears to offer no clear benefit. This means that a wide array of people (including volunteers and college students) can succeed with proper training and support.

Given these parameters, a Rethinker sees a raft of promising possibilities.

One is to try to match student needs to available tools. If students need assistance with early literacy or math operations, there are powerful online tutorials that can help. While schools may have trouble arranging (or affording) ninety minutes a week of in-person tutoring, these resources can help ease that problem. Computer-assisted tutoring may not be as effective as the best human tutors, but it's accessible, reliable, and pretty effective at teaching basic skills.

It's not surprising that out-of-school tutoring is less effective than tutoring during the school day, especially when we consider the logistical challenges and potential distractions. But finding ninety minutes a week during school can be an impossible task today, *especially* for schools struggling to find enough staff. Rather than proceeding haphazardly, with teachers expected to "just make it work," a Rethinker is inclined to reexamine the school schedule and the duties of staff. (If this makes change slower or more difficult, they know that that's the difference between one more slapdash gesture and a solution that might actually deliver.)

Research has also suggested the promise of intensive "vacation academy" programs in which groups of struggling students devote a weeklong break to a single subject. With student-teacher ratios of roughly 10 to 1, these programs are relatively inexpensive, but they're also more akin to classroom teaching. That means they really call for experienced teachers. School calendars or hybrid homeschool models can incorporate the requisite time for both students and selected staff. Again, this needs to be done not with duct tape but by deliberately rethinking the calendar, school breaks, teacher roles, and teacher compensation.

Tutoring sits at the nexus of so many of the strands we've touched upon, including teaching, the use of time and technology, and the role of education options and families. But tutoring is hardly unique on this count. Most school improvement strategies—whether they emphasize social and emotional learning (SEL), differentiated instruction, career and technical education, or much else—invariably cut across most (or all) of the topics we've explored in this volume.

Rethinking is not a technical or professorial exercise; it's not about adjusting *this* dial or injecting schools with a dollop of *that*. It's a complicated, human, messy process.

Successful Rethinkers proceed accordingly.

RETHINKING THAT RESONATES

We're coming up on the end of our time together. As we do, a closing question I often hear is, "Okay, so I've some thoughts on what to do when it comes to rethinking. But there's so much anger and distrust out there. Any ideas on how we move forward in the face of *that*?"

Well, I don't have any pat answers (and I'm distrustful of those who claim they do). But I've been doing this a long time and do have a few thoughts to share. The most important is to approach rethinking *as a human endeavor and not a technical one.*

It's not about how smart you are or how clever a reform is. Parents and teachers want to know that changes will work for children and communities, that your nifty idea isn't going to cause problems, and that it was crafted with respect for the beating heart of the schoolhouse.

Rethinkers need to demonstrate that they get that. Talking like a technician signals that you don't.

Again, *that's* why the exercises throughout this volume have been designed for groups rather than individuals. That's not the norm, I know, but it reflects the Rethinker's penchant for practical deliberation rather than fanciful bouts of "Wouldn't this be cool?"

And there's more appetite for this kind of effort than the headlines might suggest. While the bitter clashes that wash over schools today are a consequence of the fractured trust that marks our polarized age, polling shows that three out of four Americans are sick of our performative fights (this is certainly consistent with my experience).[10] The problem is that the measured majority gets drowned out by the cable news loudmouths and social media screamers. Rethinking requires pushing past the high-decibel posturing to engage and empower the problem-solvers.

That means school and system leaders need to make time to talk face-to-face with concerned parents and community leaders. We're far more likely to forge trust when we interact with three-dimensional human beings, see body language, and share a laugh. It's when conversations unfold in formal board meetings or online that angry tweets and viral videos can most readily squeeze out questions and contemplation. And that's death for rethinking.

EMBRACE THE SKEPTICISM

The Rethinker's biggest challenge, as we noted in chapter 1, may be the justifiable cynicism with which so many parents and teachers have come to regard talk of school reform. Leaders will say, "I get it. People are skeptical. I have to earn their trust."

But I find that these leaders too rarely appreciate the true scope of the challenge. I've seen too many talk the talk and then just put their head down and charge into a brick wall.

The hardest thing in the world, *especially* when we're enamored by promising new ideas, is to understand why someone else may be dubious. I get it.

But the reality is that, when a new principal rises to give that rousing charge to their first faculty meeting—"This is a new day. What's come before is prologue. Everybody gets a clean slate. Etc."—that principal is usually the only one in the room who believes it. For many teachers, it's the second or third (or seventh) time they've heard that speech. They've learned to tune it out and tell each other, "This too shall pass." The same applies to every superintendent who's ever unveiled a strategic vision to a districtwide gathering of staff and school leaders.

How do you break through that? Well, you *don't* do it by insisting that *this* time, "Things really *will* be different."

Most parents and teachers have seen plenty of "transformative" education leaders, reforms, and technologies come and go. While we might wish there were a reset button to do away with all that disappointing history, the reality is that the landscape is dotted with the disillusioning detritus of once-hailed innovators (and their once-acclaimed innovations).

This is a big reason why talk of transformation, disruption, and innovation is so unhelpful. It sounds like leaders don't know or don't understand what's come before or why parents and educators may be skeptical.

Don't assume that anyone will simply agree *this* time is different. Trust has to be earned. Leaders earn it by making parents and educators feel like *their* concerns are being heard and taken seriously.

LISTEN AND LEARN

Rethinking requires parents, teachers, and policy makers to get comfortable with new possibilities. That's a tall order in a distrustful age, especially given the dismal track record of school reform.

It is, though, a challenge that education leaders should be well equipped to tackle. Educators, after all, are experienced at helping others see new things, master new ideas, and wrestle with uncomfortable questions. Heck, educators *specialize* in educating people.

Look, in schooling, we talk *a lot* about "courageous conversations." Unfortunately, these conversations too rarely live up to the name. They're often heavy on haranguing and light on listening.

And it's no great surprise that hectoring people isn't likely to open minds or surface common ground. Researchers have long known that insulting someone in the course of an argument leads them to dig in their heels.[11] This phenomenon even has a name: the "boomerang effect."[12] Meanwhile, researchers at Yale and UC Berkeley have found that deep listening is more powerful than talking when it comes to changing minds.[13]

As my old boss, Harvard University's Arthur Brooks, argues, "If you want a chance at changing minds, you need a new strategy: Stop using your values as a weapon, and start offering them as a gift."[14]

Fight the temptation to tell doubters "You're wrong!" and then just repeat your talking points, slower and louder. Instead, try to understand their concerns. Approach persuasion as a chance to more fully think through and explain what you're doing. As Brooks muses:

> I have known quite a few religious missionaries, who tend to be cheerful despite facing almost constant rejection of their closest-held values. As one told me once, "No one ever said, 'Great news: There are missionaries on the porch.'" What explains this apparent dissonance? The answer is that effective missionaries present their beliefs as a gift.[15]

There are a few practices that can help on this count.

Don't "Other" Those Who Disagree

Don't treat those who question your vision as enemies. If you're rethinking teacher roles or the use of school time, try not to turn skeptics into outcasts. Keep the lines of communication open and take every opportunity to extend a hand to those who aren't on board. This gives you a chance to build a relationship with the doubters, which can provide additional benefits over time.

Learn from the Pushback

Hesitance and reluctance are normal. They're healthy and can provide valuable cautions about how tough a given change will be. A big mistake education reformers have sometimes made in the past, with efforts like No Child Left Behind or the Common Core, is to ride roughshod over concerns. This leads us to miss out on critical information (and tends to turn fence-sitting doubters into enemies).

Listen More, Much More

One of the things I realized a couple years ago, when Pedro Noguera, dean of the University of Southern California Rossier School of Education, and

I wrote our book *A Search for Common Ground*, is how often we approach conversation as a chance to prove "I'm right" rather than as an opportunity to understand or to learn. The problem is that rehashing our usual talking points doesn't usually persuade anyone who doesn't already agree. On the other hand, learning to appreciate other views can help us find points of agreement or craft effective appeals.[16]

EVERYONE IS THE HERO OF THEIR STORY

When it comes to actually trying to do any of this, there are many lessons I've learned over the years. Perhaps the most important one is appreciating that everyone involved in schooling thinks *they're* the good guy.

Sit with a teacher, and they'll tell you how hard they work, how long their days are, how unappreciated they feel, how much energy they devote to helping their students succeed, but how often they're hampered by meddling principals.

Sit down with a principal, and they'll tell you how hard they work, how long their days are, how unappreciated they feel, how much energy they put into helping their teachers and students succeed, but how often they're hampered by the meddling clowns in the central office.

Talk to those "meddling clowns" in the central office, and they'll tell you how hard they work, how long their days are, how unappreciated they feel, how much energy they put into helping their principals, teachers, and students succeed, but how often they're hampered by irksome school boards and irate parents.

Talk to school board members or parents . . . You get the idea.

The point: *everybody* thinks *they're* the hero of the story. If you don't get that, you'll find yourself constantly wondering why these ill-intentioned people are standing in your way. But 99 percent of the time they're wondering why *you're* in *their* way. Whether it's overhauling how schools use time, reshaping the teaching job, or leveraging educational choice, those on both sides of a decision are convinced they're right.

Especially in schooling, where kids, values, and public funds are at stake, emotions run hot. Trying to win these debates by shaming or outmuscling the doubters doesn't work so well. And, even when it works short term, it can fuel a bitter backlash with time.

This points the way to more politically adroit (and effective) leadership. Parents will inevitably question changes that promise to be disruptive.

Teachers can experience proposed reforms as an attack on their profession and personal well-being.

Leaders who dismiss parental concerns as selfish or uninformed will only inflame the opposition. Those who wave away teacher concerns by insisting it's the "right" thing to do will only foster pushback.

If you appreciate that everyone thinks *their* heart is in the right place (and that *you're* the problem), it's obvious that hectoring will tend to be a dead-end strategy. So is insisting that the research indisputably proves your point (it usually doesn't) or that you're "for the kids" (meaning they must be anti-kid).

What's the alternative?

Embrace the principles of rethinking: ask why, be specific, take a deep breath, and know that a changing world may require changing solutions (while rejecting change for change's sake).

A question-driven approach to school improvement has an added benefit. When you approach this work with a fixed answer, everyone else is transformed into an ally or an opponent. They're either behind your idea or fighting it. The more you dig in, the more firmly those lines are drawn. And then all the talk about buy-in and collaboration rings hollow.

If you start by asking what's not working, though, a different dynamic becomes possible. The great thing about starting with the history (with how we got here) is that it lets everyone off the hook—and thus invites everyone in. It's no one's fault that reformers did this in 1840 or that other thing in 1910. Heck, given the needs of that time and place, what they did back then may have made good sense. But the world has changed.

This approach shifts the focus from denouncing villains to discovering opportunities. It creates room for educators and families alike to identify frustrations and potential solutions. This is why Rethinkers can succeed where would-be reformers would fail.

FINAL THOUGHTS

In the end, rethinking isn't about a prescription. It's about recognizing a moment when we might reimagine American schooling and breathe new energy into our proud tradition of public education.

The pandemic upended American life in ways we never could have imagined. It transformed relationships between parents and educators. It illuminated the importance of our schools and also where they can do far better. In all this, it also helped point a way forward.

Rethinking entails parents and schools working together to address the kinds of challenges that the pandemic laid bare: parents want more options, students to be treated as individuals, and educators to operate as professionals. And they all want schools that feel less bureaucratic and more personal.

It's easier to appreciate these concerns than to address them. And yet, it's not enough to tackle them with passion or good intentions. After all, if you take your car in for repairs and you crash because the mechanic forgot to replace your brake pads, you don't care that he meant well. You won't be unduly comforted if he tells you how much he loves cars and believes there's a better way to install brake pads. You want him to do his job.

That's the key here. We don't need more or different or urgent or innovative. We need thoughtful. Deliberate. Intentional. And effective.

The great disruption wrought by a pandemic highlighted some profound challenges that have long confronted America's schools. It has also created a remarkable opportunity for a great rethink. Here's hoping we seize it.

Notes

Preface

1. Frederick M. Hess, *Letters to a Young Education Reformer* (Cambridge, MA: Harvard Education Press, 2017), 9.
2. Charles M. Payne, *So Much Reform, So Little Change: The Persistence of Failure in Urban Schools* (Cambridge, MA: Harvard Education Press, 2013).

Chapter 1

1. "Return to Learn Enrollment Tracker: 2020–2022," American Enterprise Institute, https://www.returntolearntracker.net/2020-22-enrollment-changes/.
2. Brian M. Stecher et al., *Improving Teaching Effectiveness: Final Report: The Intensive Partnerships for Effective Teaching Through 2015–2016* (Santa Monica, CA: RAND Corporation, 2018): xxxvi–xlii, doi:10.7249/RR2242.
3. Tom Loveless, *Between the State and the Schoolhouse: Understanding the Failure of Common Core* (Cambridge, MA: Harvard Education Press, 2021).
4. Lisa Dragoset et al., *School Improvement Grants: Implementation and Effectiveness* (Washington, DC: National Center for Education Evaluation and Regional Assistance, Institute of Education Sciences, US Department of Education, 2017), https://ies.ed.gov/ncee/pubs/20174013/pdf/20174013.pdf.
5. David B. Tyack and William Tobin, "The 'Grammar' of Schooling: Why Has It Been So Hard to Change?," *American Educational Research Journal* 31, no. 3 (1994): 453–79, doi:10.2307/1163222.
6. *The Nation's Report Card: Results from the 2019 Mathematics and Reading Assessments* (Washington, DC: US Department of Education, Institute of Education Sciences, National Center for Education Statistics, National Assessment of Educational Progress, 2019), 2, https://www.nationsreportcard.gov/mathematics/supportive_files/2019_infographic.pdf.
7. Office of the US Surgeon General, "Protecting Youth Mental Health: The U.S. Surgeon General's Advisory," US Department of Health and Human Services, December 7, 2021, https://www.hhs.gov/sites/default/files/surgeon-general-youth-mental-health-advisory.pdf; Maria Elizabeth Loades et al., "Rapid Systemic Review: The Impact of Social Isolation and Loneliness on the Mental Health of Children and Adolescents in the Context of COVID-19," *Journal of the American Academy of Child and Adolescent Psychiatry* 59, no. 11 (2020): 1218–39, doi:10.1016/j.jaac.2020.05.009.
8. Morgan Polikoff, "Parent Dissatisfaction Shows Need to Improve School Communication During Coronavirus Pandemic," *Brown Center Chalkboard* (blog), Brookings, July 23, 2020, https://www.brookings.edu/blog/brown-center-chalkboard/2020/07/23/parent

-dissatisfaction-shows-need-to-improve-school-communication-during-coronavirus
-pandemic/.

9. Ronald Heifetz, *Leadership Without Easy Answers* (Cambridge, MA: Harvard University Press, 1998). Ronald Heifetz of Harvard Kennedy School has written at length about the distinction I'm making here; he tends to talk about "adaptive leadership" versus "technical answers." As he frames it, adaptive leadership is less focused on answers than on getting key parties focused on tackling the right questions. He's used the metaphor of "being on the balcony" to describe the act of stepping back from the chaotic particulars in order to see the big picture.

10. "Total and Current Expenditures per Pupil in Public Elementary and Secondary Schools: Selected Years, 1919–20 Through 2016–17," National Center for Education Statistics, https://nces.ed.gov/programs/digest/d19/tables/dt19_236.55.asp?current=yes.

11. Benjamin Scafidi, *Back to the Staffing Surge: The Great Teacher Salary Stagnation and the Decades-Long Employment Growth in American Public Schools* (Indianapolis: EdChoice, 2017), https://www.edchoice.org/wp-content/uploads/2017/06/Back-to-the-Staffing -Surge-by-Ben-Scafidi.pdf.

12. Frederick M. Hess, *Spinning Wheels: The Politics of Urban School Reform* (Washington, DC: Brookings Institution Press, 1998).

13. David B. Tyack and Larry Cuban, *Tinkering toward Utopia: A Century of Public School Reform* (Cambridge, MA: Harvard University Press, 1995), 40–41.

14. Julie Jargon, "Parents Are the New Remote-School Zoom Bombers," *Wall Street Journal*, October 27, 2020, https://www.wsj.com/articles/parents-are-the-new-remote-school -zoom-bombers-11603800001.

15. David M. Houston, Paul E. Peterson, and Martin R. West, "Partisan Rifts Widen, Perceptions of School Quality Decline: Results of the 2022 Education Next Survey of Public Opinion," *Education Next*, August 16, 2022, https://www.educationnext.org/ partisan-rifts-widen-perceptions-school-quality-decline-results-2022-education-next -survey-public-opinion/.

16. John Kristof, "The Top 10 Findings from EdChoice's 2021 Schooling in America Survey," *ENGAGE by EdChoice*, September 2, 2021, https://www.edchoice.org/engage/the-top -10-findings-from-edchoices-2021-schooling-in-america-survey/.

17. Michael B. Henderson et al., "Hunger for Stability Quells Appetite for Change: Results of the 2021 Education Next Survey of Public Opinion," *Education Next*, August 31, 2021, https://www.educationnext.org/hunger-for-stability-quells-appetite-for-change-results -2021-education-next-survey-public-opinion-poll/.

18. Eric Wearne, *Defining Hybrid Homeschools in America: Little Platoons* (Lanham, MD: Lexington Books, 2020).

19. Drew Jacobs and Debbie Veney, *Voting With Their Feet: A State-Level Analysis of Public Charter School and District Public School Trends* (Washington, DC: National Alliance for Public Charter Schools, 2021), https://www.publiccharters.org/sites/default/files/ documents/2021-09/napcs_voting_feet_rd6.pdf; Kathleen Porter-Magee, Annie Smith, and Matt Klausmeier, "Catholic School Enrollment Boomed During Covid. Let's Make It More Than a One-Time Bump," Manhattan Institute, June 23, 2022, https://www .manhattan-institute.org/catholic-school-enrollment-boomed-during-covid; "Return to Learn Enrollment Tracker: 2020–2022."

20. For a fuller narrative that provides links to many complementary historical resources, check out the book I wrote on all this: Frederick M. Hess, *The Same Thing Over and Over:*

How School Reformers Get Stuck in Yesterday's Ideas (Cambridge, MA: Harvard University Press, 2010).

21. Sarah Pruitt, "When the Sears Catalog Sold Everything from Houses to Hubcaps," History.com, October 16, 2018, https://www.history.com/news/sears-catalog-houses -hubcaps#:~:text=Before%20there%20was%20Amazon.com,underwear%20to%20 entire%20house%20kits.

22. Frederick M. Hess, *Education Unbound: The Promise and Practice of Greenfield Schooling* (Alexandria, VA: ASCD, 2010). If you're curious about the notion of "unbundling," which is an idea that's more familiar in high tech and higher education than in K–12, I wrote about it at some length more than a decade ago in chapter 1 of *Education Unbound*.

23. Frederick M. Hess, *Cage-Busting Leadership* (Cambridge, MA: Harvard Education Press, 2013).

24. G.K. Chesterton, *The Thing* (New York, NY: Dodd, Mead & Company, 1929).

Chapter 2

1. *Prisoners of Time: Report of the National Education Commission on Time and Learning* (Denver: Education Commission of the States, 1994), https://www.ecs.org/clearinghouse /64/52/6452.pdf.

2. "How Local Educators Plan to Spend Billions in Federal Covid Aid," FutureEd, June 7, 2022, https://www.future-ed.org/local-covid-relief-spending/.

3. Evie Blad, "Why Schools See Extra Time as the Solution to Making Up for Lost Instruction," *Education Week*, March 22, 2022, https://www.edweek.org/leadership/why -schools-see-extra-time-as-the-solution-to-making-up-for-lost-instruction/2022/03.

4. Doug Lemov, *Teach Like a Champion* (San Francisco: Jossey-Bass, 2010), 7.

5. Doug Lemov, *Teach Like a Champion 3.0* (San Francisco: Jossey-Bass, 2021), 261.

6. See, for example, "Instructional Time Policies: 50-State Comparison," Education Commission of the States, last modified January 2020, https://reports.ecs.org/ comparisons/instructional-time-policies-01.

7. Elena Silva, Taylor White, and Thomas Toch, *The Carnegie Unit: A Century-Old Standard in a Changing Educational Landscape* (Stanford, CA: Carnegie Foundation for the Advancement of Teaching, 2015), 7, https://www.carnegiefoundation.org/wp-content /uploads/2015/01/Carnegie_Unit_Report.pdf.

8. Silva et al., *The Carnegie Unit*, 9.

9. David B. Tyack and Larry Cuban, *Tinkering Toward Utopia: A Century of Public School Reform* (Cambridge, MA: Harvard University Press, 1995), 93.

10. Kenneth Gold, *School's In: The History of Summer Education in American Public Schools* (New York: Peter Lang, 2002).

11. Gold, *School's In*.

12. Valerie Strauss, "Report Busts Myth That U.S. Class Time Is Much Lower Than That of High-Performing Nations," *Washington Post*, December 13, 2011, https://img.washing-tonpost.com/blogs/answer-sheet/post/report-busts-myth-that-us-class-time-is-much -lower-than-that-of-high-performing-nations/2011/12/12/gIQAtf2dqO_blog.html.

13. "Table 1.1. Minimum Number of Instructional Days and Hours in the School Year, Minimum Number of Hours Per School Day, and School Start/Finish Dates, by State: 2020," National Center for Education Statistics, 2020, https://nces.ed.gov/programs/ statereform/tab1_1-2020.asp.

14. Jennifer Craw, "Statistic of the Month: How Much Time Do Students Spend in School?," National Center on Education and the Economy, February 22, 2018, https://ncee.org/quick-read/statistic-of-the-month-how-much-time-do-students-spend-in-school/.

15. Craw, "Statistic of the Month."

16. OECD, *Education at a Glance 2021: OECD Indicators* (Paris, France: OECD Publishing, 2021), 342, doi:10.1787/19991487.

17. Craw, "Statistic of the Month."

18. Andrew D. Catt, *Commuting Concerns: A Survey of U.S. Parents on K–12 Transportation Before and During the COVID-19 Pandemic* (Indianapolis: EdChoice, 2020), 8, https://files.eric.ed.gov/fulltext/ED609382.pdf.

19. Catt, *Commuting Concerns*, 15.

20. Samuel E. Abrams, "The Mismeasure of Teaching Time" (working paper, Center for Benefit-Cost Studies of Education, Teachers College, Columbia University, 2015).

21. Abrams, "The Mismeasure of Teaching Time," 11.

22. Matthew A. Kraft and Manuel Monti-Nussbaum, "The Big Problem with Little Interruptions to Classroom Learning," *AERA Open* 7, no. 1 (2021): 2, doi:10.1177/23328584211028856.

23. Kraft and Monti-Nussbaum, "The Big Problem," 8.

24. Kraft and Monti-Nussbaum, "The Big Problem," 10.

25. Frederick M. Hess and Brendan Bell, "Thanks to One Reform, School Principals Spend Weeks Doing Paperwork," *National Review*, September 7, 2017, https://www.nationalreview.com/2017/09/education-reform-wrong-way-nevada-principals-spend-weeks-doing-paperwork/.

26. Hess and Bell, "Thanks to One Reform."

27. Jodie L. Roth et al., "What Happens During the School Day? Time Diaries from a National Sample of Elementary School Teachers," *Teachers College Record* 105, no. 3 (2003): 317–43, doi:10.1111/1467-9620.00242.

28. *NAIS Report on the 2016 High School Survey of Student Engagement* (Washington, DC: NAIS, 2017), https://www.fcis.org/uploaded/Data_Reports/2016-HSSSE_Final_1.pdf.

29. See, for example, Devin Bodkin, "Surveys Display Highs and Lows of Student Engagement," *Idaho Ed News*, August 17, 2021, https://www.idahoednews.org/news/surveys-display-highs-and-lows-of-student-engagement/; EdWeek Research Center, "Data Snapshot: What Teacher and Student Morale Looks Like Right Now," *Education Week*, January 6, 2021, https://www.edweek.org/leadership/data-snapshot-what-teacher-and-student-morale-looks-like-right-now/2021/01.

30. EdWeek Research Center, "Data Snapshot."

31. "Learning from Student Voice: Are Students Engaged," YouthTruth, 2017, https://youthtruthsurvey.org/student-engagement/.

32. Brandon Busteed, "The School Cliff: Student Engagement Drops with Each School Year," *Gallup Blog*, January 7, 2013, https://news.gallup.com/opinion/gallup/170525/school-cliff-student-engagement-drops-school-year.aspx.

33. Heidi E. Parker, *Digital Badges as Effective Assessment Tools* (Urbana: University of Illinois and Indiana University, National Institute for Learning Outcomes Assessment, 2015), 2–3, https://www.learningoutcomesassessment.org/wp-content/uploads/2019/04/AiP_Parker.pdf.

34. Parker, *Digital Badges*.

35. Victor Gonzalez, "Digital Badges: Recognizing Learning," *Leadership Magazine*, January 2015, https://cdn5-ss18.sharpschool.com/UserFiles/Servers/Server_211876/File/Our%

20Departments/Educational%20Services/Curriculum%20&%20Instruction/PASSPORT
%20TO%20SUCCESS/Digital%20Badge%20Summer%20Institutes/Article%20from%
20Leadership%20magazine%20Jan-Feb%202015%20V%2044%20No%203.pdf.

36. Henry D. Thoreau, *Walden* (Boston: Ticknor and Fields, 1854).
37. Arthur C. Brooks, "Stop Spending Time on Things You Hate," *Atlantic*, April 29, 2021, https://www.theatlantic.com/family/archive/2021/04/waste-time-thoreau-walden /618732/.
38. Cal Newport, *Deep Work: Rules for Focused Success in a Distracted Word* (New York: Grand Central Publishing, 2016).

Chapter 3

1. Lisa Chu and Bree Dusseault, "Analysis: Data from 100 Large Urban Districts Show Half Facing Shortages in Key Positions. Fixing That Will Mean Rethinking Teaching & Working in Schools," *The 74*, March 23, 2022, https://www.the74million.org/article/chu -dusseault-half-of-100-large-urban-districts-have-serious-staffing-shortages-fixing-that -means-rethinking-teaching-and-working-in-schools/.
2. Katherine Fung, "Aging Teacher Workforce Further Whittled Down by Pandemic Staff Shortage," *Newsweek*, January 3, 2022, https://www.newsweek.com/aging-teacher -workforce-further-whittled-down-pandemic-staff-shortage-1664341; Chu and Dusseault, "Analysis: Data From 100 Large Urban Districts."
3. Chad Aldeman and Ashley LiBetti Mitchel, *No Guarantees: Is it Possible to Ensure Teachers Are Ready on Day One?* (Washington, DC: Bellwether Education Partners, 2016), https://bellwethereducation.org/sites/default/files/Bellwether_NoGuarantees _Final.pdf.
4. Kwang Suk Yoon et al., *Reviewing the Evidence on How Teacher Professional Development Affects Student Achievement* (Washington, DC: US Department of Education, Institute of Education Sciences, National Center for Education Evaluation and Regional Assistance, Regional Educational Laboratory Southwest, 2007), https://ies.ed.gov/ncee/edlabs /regions/southwest/pdf/rel_2007033.pdf.
5. Stephen Sawchuk, "Review Finds Few Impacts for Math Professional Development," *Education Week*, February 13, 2014, https://www.edweek.org/leadership/review -finds-few-impacts-for-math-professional-development/2014/02.
6. Tom Loveless, "What Do We Know About Professional Development," Brookings, February 19, 2014, https://www.brookings.edu/research/what-do-we-know-about -professional-development/.
7. Maya Riser-Kositsky, "School Staffing by the Numbers," *Education Week*, June 15, 2021, https://www.edweek.org/leadership/school-staffing-by-the-numbers/2022/06.
8. "Table 1. National Employment and Wage Data from the Occupational Employment and Wage Statistics Survey by Occupation, May 2021," US Bureau of Labor Statistics, May 2021, https://www.bls.gov/news.release/ocwage.t01.htm.
9. Ashley Kincaid, "The Evidence is Mounting: Teacher Specialization in Elementary Grades Hurts Student Learning," *National Council on Teacher Quality* (blog), February 24, 2022, https://www.nctq.org/blog/The-evidence-is-mounting:-Teacher-specialization -in-elementary-grades-hurts-student-learning.
10. *1st Annual Merrimack College Teacher Survey: 2022 Results* (Bethesda, MD: EdWeek Research Center, Merrimack College, 2022), https://fs24.formsite.com/edweek/images/ WP-Merrimack_College-Todays_Teachers_Are_Deeply_Disillusioned_Survey_Data _Confirms.pdf.

11. Holly Kurtz, "A Profession in Crisis: Findings From a National Teacher Survey," *Education Week*, April 14, 2022, https://www.edweek.org/research-center/reports/teaching-profession-in-crisis-national-teacher-survey.

12. OECD, *Education at a Glance 2021: OECD Indicators* (Paris, France: OECD Publishing, 2021), 380, doi:10.1787/19991487.

13. *Multi-Classroom Leadership: School Model* (Chapel Hill, NC: Opportunity Culture, Public Impact, 2012/2018), https://opportunityculture.org/wp-content/uploads/2012/04/Multi-Classroom_Leadership_School_Model-Public_Impact.pdf.

14. Carole G. Basile and Brent W. Maddin, *The Next Education Workforce: Team-Based Staffing Models Can Make Schools Work Better for Both Learners and Educators* (Washington, DC: American Enterprise Institute, 2022), https://www.aei.org/wp-content/uploads/2022/07/The-Next-Education-Workforce.pdf?x91208.

15. Madeline Will, "Teacher Salaries Aren't Keeping Up With Inflation. See How Your State Compares," *Education Week*, April 26, 2022, https://www.edweek.org/teaching-learning/teacher-salaries-arent-keeping-up-with-inflation-see-how-your-state-compares/2022/04; *Rankings of the States 2021 and Estimates of School Statistics 2022* (Washington, DC: National Education Association Research, 2022), 5, https://www.nea.org/sites/default/files/2022-06/2022%20Rankings%20and%20Estimates%20Report.pdf.

16. Benjamin Scafidi, *Back to the Staffing Surge: The Great Teacher Salary Stagnation and the Decades-Long Employment Growth in American Public Schools* (Indianapolis: EdChoice, 2017), https://www.edchoice.org/wp-content/uploads/2017/06/Back-to-the-Staffing-Surge-by-Ben-Scafidi.pdf.

17. Scafidi, *Back to the Staffing Surge*, 2.

18. Scafidi, *Back to the Staffing Surge*, 5.

19. *Rankings of the States 2021 and Estimates of School Statistics 2022*.

20. "Admissions," National Council on Teacher Quality, 2021, https://www.nctq.org/review/standard/Admissions.

21. Thomas J. Kane, Jonah E. Rockoff, and Douglas O. Staiger, "Photo Finish: Teacher Certification Doesn't Guarantee a Winner" *Education Next* 7, no. 1. (2007), https://www.educationnext.org/photo-finish/.

22. *Students', Teachers', and Administrators' Attitudes towards High School and School Reform* (Washington, DC: Aspen Institute, 2005), https://www.aspeninstitute.org/wp-content/uploads/files/content/docs/education/educationteacherviews.pdf.

23. Madeline Will, "States Relax Teacher Certification Rules to Combat Shortages," *Education Week*, June 28, 2022, https://www.edweek.org/teaching-learning/states-relax-teacher-certification-rules-to-combat-shortages/2022/06.

24. Frederick M. Hess, "Tennessee's Pioneering Teacher Apprenticeship Program," *Forbes*, January 19, 2022, https://www.forbes.com/sites/frederickhess/2022/01/19/tennessees-pioneering-teacher-apprenticeship-program/?sh=46445c9dab42.

25. Richard Rusczyk, interview by Rick Hess, "Straight Up Conversation: Math Guru Richard Rusczyk," *Rick Hess Straight Up* (blog), *Education Week*, April 19, 2018, https://www.edweek.org/education/opinion-straight-up-conversation-math-guru-richard-rusczyk/2018/04.

Chapter 4

1. Larry Cuban, *Oversold and Underused: Computers in the Classroom* (Cambridge, MA: Harvard University Press, 2001).

2. Pictures of the Past, "Formula 1 Pit Stops 1950 & Today," YouTube video, 2:09, April 12, 2014, https://www.youtube.com/watch?v=RRy_73ivcms.

3. Larry Cuban, *Teachers and Machines: The Classroom Use of Technology Since 1920* (New York: Teachers College Press, 1986), 9, 12.

4. The US Department of Education did not exist until October 1979, when it was created by Congress during Jimmy Carter's presidency.

5. Cuban, *Teachers and Machines*, 19, 25; L. Paul Saettler, *The Evolution of American Educational Technology*, 2nd ed. (Charlotte, NC: Information Age Publishing, 2004), 198.

6. Cuban, *Teachers and Machines*, 28, 39.

7. Diane Curtis, "A Computer for Every Lap: The Maine Learning Technology Initiative," *Edutopia*, May 12, 2003, https://www.edutopia.org/stw-maine-project-based-learning -technology-initiative.

8. Michael B. Horn, "No Shock as Peru's One-to-One Laptops Miss Mark," *Forbes*, August 22, 2012, https://www.forbes.com/sites/michaelhorn/2012/08/22/no-shock-as-perus-one -to-one-laptops-miss-mark/?sh=19936ae278d4; "Peru's Ambitious Laptop Program Gets Mixed Grades," *eSchool News*, July 3, 2012, https://www.eschoolnews.com/2012/07/03 /perus-ambitious-laptop-program-gets-mixed-grades/.

9. Alyson Klein, "Tech Fatigue Is Real for Teachers and Students. Here's How to Ease the Burden," *Education Week*, March 8, 2022, https://www.edweek.org/technology /tech-fatigue-is-real-for-teachers-and-students-heres-how-to-ease-the-burden/2022/03#: ~:text=And%2079%20percent%20said%20they,their%20teachers%20some% 20breathing%20room.

10. V. Darleen Opfer, Julia H. Laufman, and Lindsey E. Thompson, *Implementation of K–12 State Standards for Mathematics and English Language Arts and Literacy: Findings from the American Teacher Panel* (Santa Monica, CA: RAND Corporation, 2017), 38–40, https://www.rand.org/content/dam/rand/pubs/research_reports/RR1500/RR1529-1 /RAND_RR1529-1.pdf.

11. Opfer et al., *Implementation of K–12 State Standards for Mathematics and English Language Arts and Literacy*, 26–28.

12. Clayton M. Christensen et al. "Know Your Customers' 'Jobs to Be Done,'" *Harvard Business Review*, September 2016, https://hbr.org/2016/09/know-your-customers-jobs -to-be-done.

13. Thomas Arnett, "Why Aren't Teachers Using the Resources Companies Sell to Their Districts?" in *Rethinking K–12 Education Procurement: Why Promising Programs, Practices, and Products Seem to Rarely Get Adopted, Implemented, or Used*, ed. Frederick M. Hess (Washington, DC: American Enterprise Institute, 2021), 10, https://www.aei.org/ wp-content/uploads/2021/02/BK-Rethinking-K12-Education-Procurement_online .pdf?x91208.

14. Ekaterina Novoseltseva, "User-Centered Design: An Introduction," https://usabilitygeek. com/user-centered-design-introduction/#:~:text=What%20is%20User%2DCentered%20 Design,user's%20requirements%2C%20objectives%20and%20feedback.

15. Frederick M. Hess, "The Company Crowdsourcing Homework Help," *Rick Hess Straight Up* (blog), *Education Week*, July 14, 2021, https://www.edweek.org/technology/opinion -the-company-crowdsourcing-homework-help/2021/07.

16. Theodore R. Sizer, *Horace's School: Redesigning the American High School* (New York: Mariner Books, 1997).

17. Ave Rio, "Virtual Reality: Bringing the Future Forward," *Chief Learning Officer*, March 8, 2018, https://www.chieflearningofficer.com/2018/03/08/virtual-reality-bringing-future -forward/.

18. Mandy Erickson, "Virtual Reality System Helps Surgeons, Reassures Patients," *Stanford*

Medicine, July 11, 2017, https://med.stanford.edu/news/all-news/2017/07/virtual-reality -system-helps-surgeons-reassures-patients.html.

19. Ramona Schindelheim, "ASU's Dreamscape Learn: How Virtual Reality is Transforming Education," *WorkingNation*, December 30, 2021, https://workingnation.com/ asus-dreamscape-learn-how-virtual-reality-is-transforming-education/.

20. Marina Umaschi Bers, *Beyond Coding: How Children Learn Human Values Through Programming* (Cambridge, MA: MIT Press, 2022).

21. Frederick M. Hess, "Silicon Schools CEO Offers Hard-Earned Lessons on Remote Learning," *Rick Hess Straight Up* (blog), *Education Week*, February 4, 2021, https://www .edweek.org/leadership/opinion-silicon-schools-ceo-offers-hard-earned-lessons-on -remote-learning/2021/02.

22. Hess, "Silicon Schools CEO Offers Hard-Earned Lessons."

23. Jonathan Haidt and Jean M. Twenge, "This is Our Chance to Pull Teenagers Out of the Smartphone Trap," *New York Times*, July 31, 2021, https://www.nytimes.com/2021/07/31 /opinion/smartphone-iphone-social-media-isolation.html.

24. Jean M. Twenge, "Have Smartphones Destroyed a Generation?" *Atlantic*, September 2017, https://www.theatlantic.com/magazine/archive/2017/09/has-the-smartphone -destroyed-a-generation/534198/.

25. Georgia Wells, Jeff Horwitz, and Deepa Seetharaman, "Facebook Knows Instagram Is Toxic for Teen Girls, Company Documents Show," *Wall Street Journal*, September 14, 2021, https://www.wsj.com/articles/facebook-knows-instagram-is-toxic-for-teen-girls -company-documents-show-11631620739?mod=hp_lead_pos7&mod=article_inline; "The Facebook Files: A Wall Street Journal Investigation," *Wall Street Journal*, https:// www.wsj.com/articles/the-facebook-files-11631713039; "Facebook's Documents About Instagram and Teens, Published," *Wall Street Journal*, September 29, 2021, https://www .wsj.com/articles/facebook-documents-instagram-teens-11632953840.

26. Jean M. Twenge et al., "Worldwide Increases in Adolescent Loneliness," *Journal of Adolescence* 93 (2021), doi:10.1016/j.adolescence.2021.06.006.

27. Jean M. Twenge, *iGen: Why Today's Super-Connected Kids Are Growing Up Less Rebellious, More Tolerant, Less Happy—and Completely Unprepared for Adulthood—and What That Means for the Rest of Us* (New York: Atria Books, 2017), 51.

28. Victoria Rideout and Michael B. Robb, *The Common Sense Census: Media Use by Tweens and Teens* (San Francisco: Common Sense Media, 2019), 23, https://www .commonsensemedia.org/sites/default/files/research/report/2019-census-8-to-18-full -report-updated.pdf.

29. Jason M. Nagata et al., "Screen Time Use Among US Adolescents During the COVID-19 Pandemic: Findings From the Adolescent Brain Cognitive Development (ABCD) Study," *JAMA Pediatrics* 176, no. 1 (2022): 94–96, doi:10.1001/jamapediatrics.2021.4334.

30. Christopher H. Lovelock and Robert F. Young, "Look to Consumers to Increase Productivity," *Harvard Business Review*, May 1979, https://hbr.org/1979/05/look-to -consumers-to-increase-productivity.

Chapter 5

1. *The Public, Parents, and K—12 Education National Polling Report: July 2022* (Indianapolis: EdChoice, Morning Consult, 2022), 23, 47, 51, 55, https://edchoice .morningconsultintelligence.com/assets/172931.pdf; *National Tracking Poll #2207087: July 14–15, 2022 Crosstabulation Results* (Indianapolis: EdChoice, Morning Consult, 2022), 78–80, https://edchoice.morningconsultintelligence.com/assets/173977.pdf.

2. "New Poll: School Choice Support at All-Time High," American Federation for Children, June 29, 2021, https://www.federationforchildren.org/new-poll-school-choice-support -at-all-time-high/; Megan Brenan, "K–12 Parents Remain Largely Satisfied with Child's Education," Gallup, August 26, 2021, https://news.gallup.com/poll/354083/parents -remain-largely-satisfied-child-education.aspx.

3. Arthur G. Powell, Eleanor Farrar, and David K. Cohen, *The Shopping Mall High School: Winners and Losers in the Educational Marketplace* (Boston: Houghton Mifflin Harcourt, 1985).

4. Drew Catt, John Kristof, and Colyn Ritter, *2022 Schooling in America* (Indianapolis: EdChoice, 2022), 21, https://www.edchoice.org/wp-content/uploads/2022/11/2022-SIA-powerpoint-FOR-WEB-3-FIXED.pdf.

5. Ashley Jochim and Jennifer Poon, *Crisis Breeds Innovation: Pandemic Pods and the Future of Education* (Tempe: Center on Reinventing Public Education, Arizona State University, 2022), https://crpe.org/wp-content/uploads/CRPE-Pandemic-Pods-Report_Pages _FINAL.pdf.

6. Jochim and Poon, *Crisis Breeds Innovation*.

7. Jochim and Poon, *Crisis Breeds Innovation*.

8. Steven Weiner, "Pandemic Learning Pod Instructors Loved Teaching, but Don't Want to be Traditional Classroom Teachers," Center on Reinventing Public Education, October 2021, https://crpe.org/pandemic-learning-pod-instructors-loved-teaching-but-dont -want-to-be-traditional-classroom-teachers/.

9. Weiner, "Pandemic Learning Pod Instructors."

10. Weiner, "Pandemic Learning Pod Instructors."

11. Ashley Jochim and Jennifer Poon, "Pandemic Pods Show the Value of Designing for Individual Needs. Will We Learn From Them?," Center on Reinventing Public Education, April 2021, https://crpe.org/pandemic-pods-show-the-value-of-designing-for -individual-needs-will-we-learn-from-them/.

12. To appreciate how some of this is playing out in the nation's largest school system, it's worth perusing this report. See Juliet Squire, *Small Schools in the Big Apple: How State-Level Policy Inhibits Microschooling and Learning Pods* (New York: Manhattan Institute, 2021), https://media4.manhattan-institute.org/sites/default/files/MI_NY _microschooling_squire.pdf.

13. Juliet Squire, *Charter Teachers' to Expand Choice and Transform Schooling* (Washington, DC: American Enterprise Institute, 2020), https://www.aei.org/research-products/report /charter-teachers-to-expand-choice-and-transform-schooling/.

14. Dave Dentel, "Census Data Shows Phenomenal Homeschool Growth," Home School Legal Defense Association, April 1, 2021, https://hslda.org/post/census-data-shows -phenomenal-homeschool-growth.

15. *The Views of Special Education Parents: Schooling Experiences and Opinions during the COVID-19 Pandemic* (Indianapolis: EdChoice, Morning Consult, 2022), 17, https:// edchoice.morningconsultintelligence.com/assets/154309.pdf#page=17.

16. *The Views of Special Education Parents*, 32.

17. Michael Q. McShane, *Hybrid Homeschooling: A Guide to the Future of Education* (Lanham, MD: Rowman & Littlefield, 2021).

18. Mike McShane, interview by Rick Hess, "Is Hybrid Home Schooling the Future of Education?" *Rick Hess Straight Up* (blog), *Education Week*, April 15, 2021, https://www .edweek.org/policy-politics/opinion-is-hybrid-home-schooling-the-future-of-education /2021/04.

19. Jocelyn Pickford and Duncan Robb, *Microschooling in Idaho: Using Policy to Scale a New Type of Small-School Environment* (New York: Manhattan Institute, 2021), https://media4 .manhattan-institute.org/sites/default/files/MI-pickfor-robb-ID.pdf.

20. *Part-Time Enrollment: Policy Analysis* (Tallahassee, FL: ExcelinEd, 2021), 1, https:// excelined.org/wp-content/uploads/2021/06/ExcelinEd_PolicyAnalysis_PartTime Enrollment_June2021.pdf.

21. McShane, interview by Rick Hess, "Is Hybrid Home Schooling the Future of Education?"

22. Brenan, "K–12 Parents."

23. Frank Edelblut, interview by Rick Hess, "How New Hampshire High Schoolers Can Earn Credits Essentially Anywhere," *Education Next Blog*, January 31, 2020, https://www. educationnext.org/how-new-hampshire-high-schoolers-can-earn-credits-essentially -anywhere-edelblut/.

24. Edelblut, "How New Hampshire High Schoolers."

25. Marco Ovidi, "Parents Know Better: Primary School Choice and Student Achievement in London" (working paper, No. 919, Queen Mary University of London, School of Economics and Finance, 2021), http://hdl.handle.net/10419/247188.

26. Thomas Stewart and Patrick J. Wolf, *The School Choice Journey: School Vouchers and the Empowerment of Urban Families* (New York: Palgrave Macmillan, 2014).

27. Stewart and Wolf, *The School Choice Journey*.

28. Frederick Hess, "Straight Up Conversation: Can Outschool Bring the Big Economy to K–12?," *Rick Hess Straight Up* (blog), *Education Week*, October 3, 2019, https://www. edweek.org/education/opinion-straight-up-conversation-can-outschool-bring-the-gig -economy-to-k-12/2019/10.

29. Erin Schulte, "How Outschool Won the Pandemic," *Fast Company*, March 11, 2022, https://www.fastcompany.com/90729413/how-outschool-won-the-pandemic #:~:text=Nathoo%20says%20Outschool%20has%20a,the%20platform%20and%20its%20 users.

Chapter 6

1. Sonya B. Santelises, "Parents Are Watching Like Never Before. 'Trust Us' Isn't Enough," *Education Week*, December 1, 2020, https://www.edweek.org/teaching-learning/opinion -parents-are-watching-like-never-before-trust-us-isnt-enough/2020/12.

2. Ashley Jochim and Jennifer Poon, *Crisis Breeds Innovation: Pandemic Pods and the Future of Education* (Tempe: Center on Reinventing Public Education, Arizona State University, 2022), https://crpe.org/wp-content/uploads/CRPE-Pandemic-Pods-Report_Pages _FINAL.pdf.

3. "2020 North Carolina Teacher Working Conditions Survey Results," Center for Optimal Learning Environments, 2020, https://2020results.asqnc.com/.

4. Carly D. Robinson et al., "Reducing Student Absenteeism in the Early Grades by Targeting Parental Beliefs," *American Educational Research Journal* 55, no. 6 (2018), doi:10.3102/0002831218772274.

5. *The Longitudinal Evaluation of School Change and Performance in Title I Schools, Volume 2: Technical Report* (Washington, DC: US Department of Education, Office of the Deputy Secretary, Planning and Evaluation Service, 2001), https://www2.ed.gov/offices/OUS /PES/esed/lescp_vol2.pdf.

6. Anna T. Henderson and Karen L. Mapp, *A New Wave of Evidence: The Impact of School, Family, and Community Connections on Student Achievement* (Austin, TX: Southwest

Educational Development Laboratory, 2002), https://sedl.org/connections/resources /evidence.pdf.

7. "Research," The Canopy, https://canopyschools.transcendeducation.org/research.

8. Jenny Curtin, Melanie Dukes, and Saskia L. Thompson, "Commentary: Not Just Recovery, But Reinvention—3 Lessons from Schools Where COVID Innovations Offer New Solutions," *The 74*, November 2, 2021, https://www.the74million.org/article/ commentary-not-just-recovery-but-reinvention-3-lessons-from-schools-where-covid -innovations-offer-new-solutions/.

9. Karen L. Mapp, *Parent Engagement Toolkit for Educators* (Boston: Boston Public Schools), https://www.bostonpublicschools.org/cms/lib/MA01906464/Centricity/Domain/112/ Pages%20from%20ParentEngagement%20ToolkitForEducatorsPart2FINALpdf.pdf.

10. Maria C. Paredes, *Academic Parent-Teacher Teams (APTT): Linking Home and School Learning* (Washington, DC: WestEd), https://www.gadoe.org/School-Improvement/ Federal-Programs/Documents/Title%20I,%20Part%20A/Geers%20%20Bearden% 20APTT%20Overview.pdf.

11. Mapp, *Parent Engagement Toolkit for Educators*.

12. Anna Hinton and Karen L. Mapp, "Feature: A Conversation with Dr. Karen Mapp, Consultant on Family Engagement," US Department of Education Office of Elementary & Secondary Education, September 7, 2011, https://oese.ed.gov/2011/09/feature-a -conversation-with-dr-karen-mapp-consultant-on-family-engagement/.

13. "Parent University," Boston Public Schools, https://www.bostonpublicschools.org/ Page/5818.

14. Robert D. Putnam, *Bowling Alone: The Collapse and Revival of American Community* (New York: Simon & Schuster, 2000).

15. "What We're Learning about Developmental Relationships," Search Institute, https:// www.search-institute.org/developmental-relationships/learning-developmental -relationships/.

16. Robert D. Putnam, *Our Kids: The American Dream in Crisis* (New York: Simon & Schuster, 2016).

17. Noam Angrist and Bruce Sacerdote, "The Social Connections that Shape Economic Prospects," *Nature* 608 (2022): 37–38, doi:10.1038/d41586-022-01843-4.

18. Julia F. Fisher and Daniel Fisher, *Who You Know: Unlocking Innovations That Expand Students' Networks* (San Francisco: Jossey-Bass, 2018).

19. Julia F. Fisher, "Fisher: Who You Know—3 Ways Schools Can Foster Competency-Based Education by Focusing on Student Relationships," *The 74*, September 16, 2019, https:// www.the74million.org/article/fisher-who-you-know-3-ways-schools-can-foster -competency-based-education-by-focusing-on-student-relationships/.

20. Yuval Levin, "It was a Mistake to Let Kids onto Social Media Sites," *New York Times*, August 5, 2022, https://www.nytimes.com/2022/08/05/opinion/social-media-parents -children.html.

21. On this question, *Teach Like a Champion* author Doug Lemov, whom we encountered in chapter 2, has made a compelling, provocative case for keeping cellphones out of school (particularly in the aftermath of the pandemic). See Doug Lemov, "Take Away Their Cellphones: So we can rewire schools for belonging and achievement," *Education Next*, August 2, 2022, https://www.educationnext.org/take-away-their-cellphones-rewire -schools-belonging-achievement/.

22. Frederick M. Hess, *Letters to a Young Education Reformer* (Cambridge, MA: Harvard Education Press, 2017), 47.

Chapter 7

1. Theodore R. Sizer, *Horace's Compromise: The Dilemma of the American High School* (New York: Houghton Mifflin, 1984).
2. Frederick M. Hess, *Cage-Busting Leadership* (Cambridge, MA: Harvard Education Press, 2013).
3. James S. Coleman, "Private Schools, Public Schools, and the Public Interest," *National Affairs*, Summer 1981, https://www.nationalaffairs.com/public_interest/detail/private -schools-public-schools-and-the-public-interest.
4. Ashley Rogers Berner, *Pluralism and American Public Education: No One Way to School*, (New York: Palgrave Macmillan, 2017).
5. Patrick J. Wolf, "Myth: Public Schools Are Necessary for a Stable Democracy," in *School Choice Myths: Setting the Record Straight in Education Freedom*, ed. Corey A. DeAngelis and Neal P. McCluskey (Washington, DC: Cato Institute, 2020), 39–58.
6. Hess, *Cage-Busting Leadership*. For those who wonder how to figure out what they can change and how to find those opportunities, check out my book *Cage-Busting Leadership*. There's too much to say to rehash it here but interested readers should find what they need there.
7. Andre Joshua Nickow, Philip Oreopoulos, and Vincent Quan, *The Transformative Potential of Tutoring for PreK–12 Learning Outcomes: Lessons from Randomized Evaluations* (Cambridge, MA: Abdul Latif Jameel Poverty Action Lab, 2020), https:// www.povertyactionlab.org/sites/default/files/publication/Evidence-Review_The -Transformative-Potential-of-Tutoring.pdf.
8. Carly D. Robinson et al., "Accelerating Student Learning with High-Dosage Tutoring," *EdResearch for Recovery*, February 2021, https://annenberg.brown.edu/sites/default/files /EdResearch_for_Recovery_Design_Principles_1.pdf; Douglas N. Harris, "Toward Policy-Relevant Benchmarks for Interpreting Effect Sizes: Combining Effects with Costs," *Educational Evaluation and Policy Analysis* 31, no. 1 (September 2008): 3–29, doi:10.3102/0162373708327524.
9. Robinson et al., "Accelerating Student Learning."
10. "The Perception Gap," More in Common, 2019, https://perceptiongap.us/.
11. Robert P. Abelson and James C. Miller, "Negative Persuasion via Personal Insult," *Journal of Experimental Social Psychology* 3, no. 4 (October 1967): 321–33, doi:10.1016/0022-1031(67)90001-7.
12. Yanni Ma and Jay D. Hmielowski, "Are You Threatening Me? Identity Threat, Resistance to Persuasion, and Boomerang Effects in Environmental Communication," *Environmental Communication* 16, no. 2 (2021): 225–42, doi:10.1080/17524032.2 021.1994442.
13. Joshua L. Kalla and David E. Broockman, "Reducing Exclusionary Attitudes through Interpersonal Conversation: Evidence from Three Field Experiments," *American Political Science Review* 114, no. 2 (2020), doi:10.1017/S0003055419000923.
14. Arthur C. Brooks, "A Gentler, Better Way to Change Minds: Stop Wielding Your Values as a Weapon and Start Offering Them as a Gift," *Atlantic*, April 7, 2022, https://www .theatlantic.com/family/archive/2022/04/arguing-with-someone-different-values/629495/.
15. Brooks, "A Gentler, Better Way to Change Minds."
16. Frederick M. Hess and Pedro A. Noguera, *A Search for Common Ground: Conversations About the Toughest Questions in K-12 Education* (New York, NY: Teachers College Press, 2021).

Acknowledgments

This book was a happy accident. And I owe a deep debt of gratitude to those who made the accident possible. In August 2021, as the nation's schools prepared to embark on a third straight year of learning disrupted by COVID-19, I heard from Jayne Fargnoli, Harvard Education Press's wily editor-in-chief, regarding a column in which I'd offered a few thoughts about how school leaders might rethink familiar routines in response to the pandemic's academic and emotional toll.

She asked if I'd considered penning a book along those lines. Well, this was a topic I'd been writing and speaking about for years. And I'd grown frustrated with self-assured, urgent calls for "reform," which amounted to doing more of the same, only harder, or flowery calls for "transformation," which were far removed from the practical challenges of the schoolhouse.

It's long seemed to me that schools just aren't designed to do much of what we ask them to do today. The proper response is not more frenzied activity but eschewing talking points in order to ask how we got here, what's changed, and whether there might be better ways to meet our challenges. That was the book I told Jayne I wanted to write. She was game. She helped me shape and sharpen that notion. And here we are. You can judge the result for yourself.

I'm thankful to all who helped me make this book a reality. First and foremost, that means my extraordinary research assistants Gabriella Lasso, Tracey Marin, RJ Martin, Hayley Sanon, Alicia Nottrott, Tracy Tilus, and Elli Lucas. I benefited mightily from their research chops, editorial feedback, extraordinary energy, and sleeves-up collaboration.

This volume benefited from conversations I've had with so many colleagues over the years. But I owe a special thanks to those friends whose thinking has especially informed parts of this book. That includes Michael Brickman, Maddie Fennell, Howard Fuller, Matt Kraft, Karen Mapp, Mike McShane, Joel Rose, Bror Saxberg, Juliet Squire, Jenna Talbot, and Patrick Wolf. And I'm deeply indebted to John Bailey, Alex Baron, Celine Coggins, Dwight Jones, Julia Rafal-Baer, and Michael Sonbert, all of whom were kind enough to read earlier versions of the manuscript and share their wisdom and expertise.

As ever, I owe the deepest appreciation to the American Enterprise Institute and its president, Robert Doar, for the support that allows me to call things as I see them, without fear or favor. I've been privileged to call AEI home for two decades. I can think of few places where I'd enjoy the intellectual freedom, support, and remarkable colleagues that AEI has provided.

I want to thank the terrific team at Harvard Education Press. I've had the honor of publishing with HEP for close to two decades now, and the relationship is one I cherish. I want to especially thank Jayne Fargnoli for her friendship and support throughout this project. This is the first book I was lucky enough to pen for HEP with Jayne at the helm; here's hoping it's the first of many.

As always, I'm indebted to my wife, Joleen, for her love, droll editorial advice, and understanding. I'm grateful to my boys, Grayson and Blake, for all the daily laughs, annoyances, smiles, and distractions that remind me why I do this work, and to my parents for so very much (with a special shout-out to my dad for his stalwart copyediting).

Finally, it goes without saying that all the mistakes, flaws, and inanities in these pages are mine and mine alone, while most of the useful bits were stolen from a long list of mentors, friends, and colleagues. But such is life.

About the Author

Frederick Hess is a senior fellow and director of education policy studies at the American Enterprise Institute. He pens *Education Week*'s *Rick Hess Straight Up* blog; is a senior contributor at *Forbes*; serves as an executive editor of *Education Next*; and has authored books including *Letters to a Young Education Reformer*, *Cage-Busting Leadership*, *The Same Thing Over and Over*, and *A Search for Common Ground* (with Pedro Noguera). Once upon a time, he taught high school social studies. Since then, he's taught at universities including Harvard, Rice, Johns Hopkins, Georgetown, the University of Virginia, and the University of Pennsylvania; been repeatedly named one of the nation's most influential figures in education policy; and become one of our foremost observers of where school improvement goes wrong, and what it takes to get it right.

Index